THRIVE U

ALEX DEMCZAK

Writer: Luke Wiersma
Cover Design: Bill Chlanda
Interior Design: Bill Chlanda
Chief Editor: Allison Lewis
Assistant Editor: David Rosman
Printed in the US
ISBN: 978-0-692-64087-6

This book is dedicated to…

I would like to thank the following people in my life who have inspired me to Thrive…

God for placing the idea of Thrive U on my heart, my fiancé Erin who has supported me through the entire process, my family Carla, Basil, and Morgan who have provided wisdom and encouragement, Joe White who encouraged me in the book writing process, Natalie Nelsen my friend and administrative assistant who saw the vision of Thrive U from the beginning, graphic designer Bill Chlanda who is one of the most talented designers I have been around. Editor Allison Lewis who has an incredibly bright future in her industry, writer Luke Wiersma, assistant editor David Rosman, award winning author Jon Gordon for writing a foreword for the book, and every single athlete and coach from across the country who has taken time out of their crazy schedules to make this book a reality.

I also would like to thank the following people and organizations for their inspiration and support…

My grandparents, all of my friends and mentors at Kanakuk, Joe White, Shay Robbins, Keith Chancey, Don Ford, pastor Jeff Nelsen, pastor Steve Patzia, pastor Lee Willis, mentor Randy Setterlund, pastor John Drage, pastor Jake Killinger, Mizzou FCA director Nathan Buxman, Mizzou FCA director Kyle Wenig, Jared Dupont, pastor Bryan Blakemore, Doug Clay, Klife director Brandon Butcher, Klife director Brandon Briscoe, Tim Tebow, Mizzou coach Gary Pinkel, Mizzou Coach Andy Hill, mentor Aaron Paterson, Coach Chad Anderson, Coach Joe Oller, professor Joseph Mazza, Phantom Ranch Bible Camp, Athletes in Action Ultimate Training Camp (UTC), Big Stuff Camps, Mizzou FCA Leadership Team, Mizzou Coach's Corner, The Cotton House, John Simpson, Ron Brown, Illinois FCA director Kevin Elliott, all my extended family, and the many others who have positively impacted my life… This book is for you,

Alex Demczak

CONTENTS

TRAINING

PREGAME

GAME

POST-GAME

FOREWORD

Jon Gordon, Author of Training Camp and The Carpenter

Do you want to be great? When I ask a team of athletes this question everyone raises their hand. It's not arrogant to feel this way. We all want to be great because God planted this desire in our heart and soul. We were never meant to be average. God created us in his likeness and image. We are called to strive for greatness, to pursue excellence, to become a master of our craft, to create what has yet to be created and honor the gifts God has given us. Martin Luther said, "The Christian shoemaker does his duty not by putting little crosses on the shoes, but by making good shoes, because God is interested in good craftsmanship."

God also loves when we step out in faith to pursue greatness. After all, Jesus said, "Even greater things than I, shall you do." Even greater things than Jesus? Are you kidding me? Talk about overwhelming. Talk about a big call and vision that requires faith. Have you noticed that God often gives you a vision that makes you feel inadequate? He gives you this desire to be great and a vision for what this greatness looks like but it often makes you feel fearful and doubtful that you'll ever achieve it. I believe God does this so we will step out in faith, seek Him on our journey and realize that we can't do it alone. It is on this path that we meet God, recognize our weakness and His strength and learn the ultimate lessons: that we can't be great without God and that in our pursuit of greatness God shapes us to become someone who can bring out the greatness in others.

That's why I love this book and am thankful you are reading it. It's not just stories of successful people who have achieved greatness. It's the faith they found on their journey and real life examples of how God carried them along the way. These writers have become someone, who in their pursuit of greatness, God is using to bring out the greatness in others, including YOU. My hope is that as you read these devotionals you will be inspired to continue on your path knowing that God has a plan for you.

A WORD FROM A COACH

Dr. Joe White, President of Kanakuk Ministries

"Very early in the morning, while it was still dark, Jesus got up, left the house and went off to a solitary place, where he prayed." Mark 1:35

I was an undersized "nose man" for the "Pre-NCAA penalized" SMU Mustangs. The University of Arkansas was a top 5 football team. The All American Center with whom I battled with all afternoon was bigger, faster, and much more talented. I was enjoying the game as much as any game I ever played. We were playing above our abilities.

Late in the game, Arkansas had driven the ball down the field to our 8 yard line behind the powerful running legs of Bill Burnett, All American candidate from Smackover, Arkansas. It was third and goal, the ball was on the 8 yard line. My job was to simply hit and hold the gap between the center and right guard. I knew 3rd and 8 would be no dive play. I knew a "toss sweep" was coming and if I wanted a piece of the tackle I best hit the gap and then FLY to the outside to find Burnett with the ball. The "toss sweep" went to the right side of the Razorback line. Our corner, safety and defensive end all got tangled up with the Arkansas blockers. I scampered outside and barely got my arms around his waist on the 8 yard line as his powerful legs were driving unhampered into pay dirt. To my embarrassment I held on from behind for 8 yards before he drug me into the end zone for the score. Sports Illustrated picked up the play and made a spectacle out of my embarrassment.

Fast forward twenty years. Bill Burnett and I had become friends…brothers in Christ. We were eating Mexican food one day together in my hometown of Branson, Missouri and laughing about "the play" and my humiliation. In his laughter, a piece of tortilla chip about the size of his middle finger got caught in Bill's throat and he began to choke… violently. He was in desperation. I quickly jumped behind him and put my arms around his waist and stuck my fist into his diaphragm. (I thought for a split second, "This is exactly where I was 20 years before as the Arkansas Razorback drug me across the goal line. Maybe I'll just let him choke to death!")

One good Heimlich jolt and the chip came flying out of his throat. I told him I should have let him die! (Just kidding.) Bill is my brother in Christ. I love him like a real brother. I cherish our all–too–few times together. When we are together we talk a little about football and A LOT about God.

That's what this book by Mizzou quarterback Alex Demczak is all about. Christian athletes, inspiring testimonies, the Bible, and a lot of straight truth about what it looks like to Thrive. I've known Alex Demczak for 5 years. We run a football camp together. Alex is as good as they get. He is sincere, visionary, unselfish and caring. I respect him as much as any college athlete I know.

I love his vision for this book. You will be a more biblical athlete after spending time in it. I recommend it whole heartedly.

HOW TO USE THIS BOOK

This book contains 100 inspiring stories written by some of the best athletes from across the country. Our hope is that if you are reading this book you are looking for more. You need more. You are sick of just getting by. You are tired of surviving. You want to Thrive. And that is why this book was created. For people like you who were not made to be average. For people who want to play their sport with a purpose. For people who want to live their life with purpose. Whether you grew up in the church, or you don't believe in God, we want Thrive U to be a resource for you to discover for yourself what it looks like to Thrive in all aspects of your life. The stories you will read in this book will be counter cultural to what you are used to hearing and will be real. We don't hold anything back. You will get raw testimonies of some of the best athletes from around the country representing around 20 sports. The athletes in this book were not randomly selected. They were chosen out of hundreds of other athletes because they represent everything this book is about. They candidly share their testimonies, trials, and triumphs on some of the biggest stages in sports.

Suggested reading options:

1. Pregame/Inspiration: Bring this book to the locker room with you and have it for when you need quick inspiration or motivation, you can read an encouraging story to lift you up.
2. 100 Day Challenge: If you really want to Thrive, take on the 100 Day Thrive Challenge! Read one page per day for the next 100 days. But be careful.... This could change your life.
3. Read with a teammate: One of the best ways to Thrive is in accountability. Buy this book for a friend and share what you are learning with each other. Decide to discuss Thrive U with your teammate once a week. If you choose this option write your teammates name below.

I hope this book can be a resource to impact you and your friends along your faith journey. Most people in this culture survive. They don't Thrive. I am challenging you to get out of your comfort zone and Thrive!

____

Your Name

____

Accountability Partner's Name

Share what you're learning by using the hashtag #ThriveU
Also, go follow Thrive U on social media at @ThriveU

Keep Thriving,

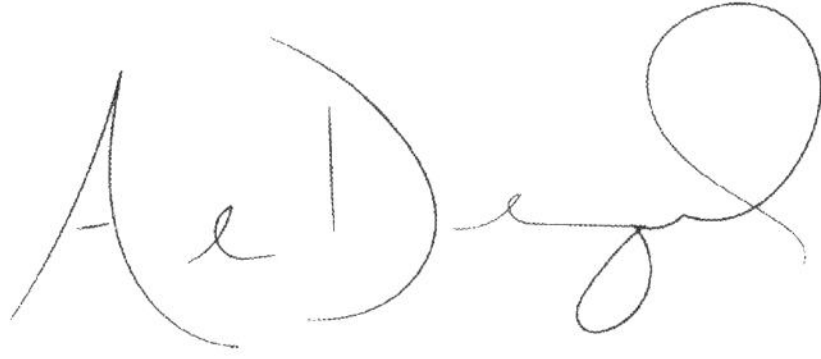

Alex Demczak

“Be strong and courageous. Do not be afraid or terrified because of them, for the LORD your God goes with you; he will never leave you nor forsake you.”

Deuteronomy 31:6

PREGAME

01

ALEX DEMCZAK

FOOTBALL

UNIVERSITY	UNIVERSITY OF MISSOURI
HOMETOWN	PLEASANT PLAINS, ILLINOIS
JERSEY	#17
POSITION	QUARTERBACK
FAVORITE ATHLETE	TIM TEBOW
FAVORITE MOVIE	FRIDAY NIGHT LIGHTS
FAVORITE ICE CREAM	BANANA SPLIT
HOBBIES	PLAYING THE DRUMS
RANDOM FACT	HASN'T HAD FRENCH FRIES SINCE 2008

A CHANGE OF PERSPECTIVE

The day that I got moved down on the team roster's depth chart changed my life. I had worked hard to improve, but when spring practice began, three new quarterbacks arrived on campus that were better than me. After a team meeting, my coach pulled me aside and told me that I would no longer get any meaningful reps in practice, to let the younger quarterbacks get experience. At the time, I didn't show outward signs of discouragement, but deep down I was crushed and felt worthless. My identity was rooted in how I performed on the football field and what people thought of me.

At this low point in my life, I pondered the thought of giving up playing football in the SEC, and decided to call a trusted friend of mine. Joe had played and coached Division 1 football and I could always count on him to give me wise advice.

I told Joe that I had been moved down on the depth chart and how embarrassed I felt. Joe told me something that I will never forget as long as I live, "Alex, this could be the best day of your life."

After a long pause I finally said, "Joe, I don't think you understand. I am 6th string on the depth chart…this is terrible!"

Then Joe said, "If you play for the approval of your coaches, football fans, or yourself, you will look back at the end of your career wishing you would have played with a purpose! Today can be the first day you actually start playing for Jesus Christ! And when you suit up for Jesus, you are always first string in his eyes!"

From that day forward, I played football differently. I trusted the Lord with my performance on the field, encouraged my teammates more (even the ones who took my spot), and focused on using the platform God gave me to be a light for other players. If you warm the bench or are an All-American, God wants to use you to bring him Glory! Make a difference today!

1. *What are some ways that I can trust God with my performance in my sport?*
2. *Who is one person that I can serve today through the way that I live and compete for Christ?*

"So, whether you eat or drink, or whatever you do, do it all for the glory of God."
1 Corinthians 10:31 (NIV)

02

ADAM HARDESTY

SOCCER

UNIVERSITY	OKLAHOMA WESLEYAN UNIVERSITY
HOMETOWN	GROVE, OKLAHOMA
JERSEY	#3
POSITION	CENTER DEFENSE
FAVORITE ATHLETE	KEVIN DURANT
FAVORITE MOVIE	REMEMBER THE TITANS
FAVORITE ICE CREAM	ROCKY ROAD
HOBBIES	FISHING, HIKING, VOLLEYBALL
RANDOM FACT	HASN'T HAD SODA SINCE AUGUST 2007

OVERCOMING ANXIETY

Anxiety has been something that I have struggled with throughout the past several years. I play soccer and going into preseason my freshman year, I was extremely anxious. On the first day we had a two mile–fitness test. I had trained all summer so that I would be in shape to compete for a starting position. While running, I was at one mile and was on pace to pass my fitness test. However, I was so nervous that I threw up. The anxiety not only caused me to get sick, but it also cost me valuable time. I finished my two miles but not with the time I was hoping for, or close to passing.

Another example of the anxiety I experienced was during the middle of my freshman season. I was not a starter nor did I have much playing time, but I continued to work hard, hoping for my chance. The starting center defender, the position I play, received a red card so the substitution players were moved up a spot. That next game, which he had to sit out, my coach told me to sub into the game. Not having much game experience at that level, I was nervous and started to worry about what would happen if I made a mistake. My concern should have been playing smart and letting my training allow me to play better. Worrying about the "what ifs" caused me to lose focus and not play to my full potential.

These are just some personal examples of how I let anxiety be in control of my life. In the book of Psalms, David wrote about his life and some of his struggles. As a king, he was in many difficult situations. Psalm 94:18-19 shows that David needed help. He had anxiety but he allowed God to still be a part of his life.

In our lives, we will have a life of regret or a life of reward; this will be decided will be based on our decisions. As student athletes, there will be times of difficulty, stress, and anxiety. Instead of worrying about what the future holds, focus on the present and the things you can control now. Give the anxiety and worry to God so He can give you peace and joy. We need to allow God to support us in every aspect of our lives.

GAME PLAN

1. *What habits can you change that will allow God to support you in your daily life?*

"When I said, 'My foot is slipping,' your unfailing love, Lord, supported me. When anxiety was great within me, your consolation brought me joy."

Psalm 94:18-19 (NIV)

03

ANDREAS PLACKIS

BASEBALL

UNIVERSITY		UNIVERSITY OF MISSOURI
HOMETOWN		ST. CHARLES, MISSOURI
JERSEY		#55
POSITION		BATS RIGHT
FAVORITE ATHLETE		ALBERT PUJOLS
FAVORITE MOVIE		THE SANDLOT
FAVORITE ICE CREAM		MINT CHOCOLATE CHIP
HOBBIES		PING PONG, READING, FAMILY TIME
RANDOM FACT		100% GREEK HERITAGE

AUDIENCE OF ONE

As athletes, we all know that working hard is a given. But the second part of Colossians 3:23 is key: " As for the Lord, and not for men." In sports, we all have audiences around us. There are a multitude of pressures pulling us in different directions, all imploring us to succeed. During my baseball career at the University of Missouri, instead of trying to please everyone, I tried to simplify things and play for one man–Jesus. Here is what this looks like.

When I step in to bat, I follow the same routine, just like 99.9 percent of the baseball playing population. I always smooth out the dirt, stretch my legs and arms, and adjust my batting gloves. Then, right before I step into the box, I always picture Jesus sitting on the outfield fence. He is my audience. I envision him out in the field as well. Because when I imagine Him sitting out there, I am reminded that I am not alone. It is Him and me, as a team, and whatever happens on the diamond should serve one purpose, to make Him more famous. This focus eliminates many of the distractions, like the peanut gallery, how good the pitcher is, whatever. It does not matter; it all boils down to just Him and me being together. I have been cheered and booed by the same fans before and I cannot play for someone who only cares about me when I do well. What would your life look like if you applied daily this same mentality on and off the field?

We cannot let God down because we do not hold Him up. He holds us up instead. When this concept hit me, I started playing with a sense of peace, a sense of freedom. No matter how I do, whether I strike out or strike it out of the park, He loves me the same. He is my audience of one.

GAME PLAN

1. *Is Jesus in your thoughts as you play?*

"Whatever you do, work at it with all your heart, as working for the Lord, not for human masters."

Colossians 3:23 (NIV)

04

AUSTIN MITCHELL

BASKETBALL

UNIVERSITY	OUACHITA BAPTIST UNIVERSITY
HOMETOWN	CONWAY, ARKANSAS
JERSEY	#15
POSITION	GUARD
FAVORITE ATHLETE	LEBRON JAMES
FAVORITE MOVIE	REMEMBER THE TITANS
FAVORITE ICE CREAM	COOKIE DOUGH
HOBBIES	SINGING, PING-PONG, EATING
RANDOM FACT	GOT TO MARRY THE LOVE OF HIS LIFE

SHORTCUTS

Off–season workouts, 6 AM runs, lifting, film room sessions, road trips and games…REPEAT.

I do not know about you, but after a while this grueling process we participate in called "sports" can be the most draining part of our life. We have been playing them since we can remember, and we could never imagine a life without them. It never ends. I can honestly say that after a while I am tempted to take shortcuts. Whether in sports or life, shortcuts come up. We just have to make sure we are prepared to make the right decision.

Shortcuts are never good but always seem to be an option throughout life. It may be not setting aside time daily with God, skipping class, skipping a set, doing one or two less reps, not touching the line. All these things will come up at some point in your life, and I know that Colossians 3:23 has been a huge help for me to make the right decision.

This verse can be applied in all parts of your life, whether it be your walk with the Lord, schoolwork, relationships, or even sports. The way I see it, Jesus did not take any shortcuts when he died on the cross for my sins, so why should I get to take shortcuts in my life? God gave me the ability to play, so why cheat Him or myself? Most things you do in sports are for your own glory, your coach, your team or to impress people. But God intended that whatever you do should be done as working for Him, not for others. That alone should give you the motivation and drive to achieve greatness.

GAME PLAN

1. *What are some ways you can avoid taking shortcuts?*
2. *Who is someone that can hold you accountable?*

"Whatever you do, work at it with all your heart, as working for the Lord, not for human masters."

Colossians 3:23 (NIV)

05

ANDREW BRILL

FOOTBALL

UNIVERSITY		TAYLOR UNIVERSITY
HOMETOWN		INDIANAPOLIS, INDIANA
JERSEY		#47
POSITION		DEFENSE END/ DEFENSE TACKLE
FAVORITE ATHLETE		JEFF SATURDAY AND REGGIE MILLER
FAVORITE MOVIE		REMEMBER THE TITANS
FAVORITE ICE CREAM		COOKIES 'N CREAM
HOBBIES		READING, BASKETBALL, PLAYING CARDS
RANDOM FACT		HAS DONE PROFESSIONAL SWING DANCING

EMPLOYER: THE LORD OUR GOD

God has blessed me greatly with the opportunity to play college football. Even more so, I was blessed by starting at defensive end my sophomore year, a rarity for an underclassman.

During this time, I created an identity of being an athlete. There was an internal struggle consisting of whether I was going to serve Jesus Christ with my ability or Andrew Brill. When I started my junior year of college, I had expected to start another year at defensive end, but when we reported to camp, we had eight defensive ends and only five defensive tackles. Due to my effectiveness against the run, my new defensive coordinator decided to switch me to a new position. This was incredibly hard for me at first because I was of the mindset that I was going to be an All–Conference starter at defensive end. In no way had I conformed or committed to the Lord's guidance.

Mentally, this was one of the hardest things that I had ever gone through in my entire athletic career. During camp, I was frustrated with myself and the coaches who had put me in this position. At the end of camp, the coaching staff showed us all a video that contained a simple message: "What's your why? Why are you not all in?" All I wanted to do was scream, "Because of the position you put me in!" But the real reason was because I had not committed my work to the Lord. I had to get on my hands and knees to realize from a very humble position that anything I do that's not for the Lord is simply not worth doing.

If God has granted you athleticism and talent, I urge you to use every bit of it for his glory! It is so easy to become trapped by the lie that our identity comes from how well we perform. But it does not; it comes from the fact that Jesus Christ is the governor of our souls. God knows more about football, soccer, hockey, tennis, cricket, or anything than the best coaches and players in the world, so why would we not only trust Him with that, but everything in our lives as well?

GAME PLAN

1. *What's your why? Why are you not all in?*

"Commit your work to the Lord, and your plans will be established."
Proverbs 16:3 (NIV)

06

CALEB ULRICH

TRACK

UNIVERSITY — COLORADO CHRISTIAN UNIVERSITY

HOMETOWN — ROANOKE, ILLINOIS

JERSEY — N/A

POSITION — N/A

FAVORITE ATHLETE — ERIC LIDDLE AND JIM RYUN

FAVORITE MOVIE — CHARIOTS OF FIRE

FAVORITE ICE CREAM — HOMEMADE VANILLA AND PEPPERMINT

HOBBIES — HUNTING AND ALL THINGS SPORTS

RANDOM FACT — HASN'T INENTIONALLY HAD MILK SINCE 2003

FALSE IDOLS

Sometimes, losing something "important" helps us realize that we have actually lost sight of the truly important things in life. After high school, I was blessed with the opportunity to run cross-country at the junior college level. The reason I say "blessed" is because I did not have the opportunity to run competitively in high school.

After a less than impressive freshman year, I was the fifth man my sophomore year in several meets for my team. We finished the regular season ranked 16th in the nation. Although my running was improving over this time, my mindset about running also changed from one of gratefulness to God for giving me an incredible opportunity, to using cross-country as a means to promote my abilities and myself.

While training for the track season early in the spring of my sophomore year, I developed an injury that forced me to miss about eight weeks of training. I had dreams of transferring into a four-year school in the fall and continuing my collegiate career. With my dreams and training on hold, I decided to attend a sports camp for college athletes hosted by a prominent Christian ministry.

One of the messages taught at camp was how, as athletes, we have a choice in using the talents God gives us. We can either use them to worship God or to worship sport, the latter being idol worship. In Jeremiah the prophet, used the example of a cracked cistern to describe what it is like to worship an idol. You constantly pour into it, but it never satisfies. This was not new information to me, but it was something that I needed to hear.

Before I left the camp that weekend, I realized that moving forward, if my running was not done from a heart of worship before God, it would never be satisfied. I think this applies not just to running or athletics in general, but to all areas of our lives. Unless, we are living them in worship to Him, we are pouring ourselves into false idols. God does not leave us helpless in the fight. He sends us His love, mercy and forgiveness each day. We are so blessed to serve and worship such an amazing God.

GAME PLAN

1. *What is an idol in your life you may be allowing to hinder your relationship with Christ?*

"My people have comitted two sins: They have forsaken me, the spring of living water, and have dug their own cisterns, broken cisterns that cannot hold water."
Jeremiah 2:13 (NIV)

07

CARLY SCHUMACHER

VOLLEYBALL

UNIVERSITY	SAINT LOUIS UNIVERSITY
HOMETOWN	CLINTON, ILLINOIS
JERSEY	#17
POSITION	MIDDLE BLOCKER
FAVORITE ATHLETE 	KERRI WALSH AND GABBIE DOUGLAS
FAVORITE MOVIE	THE BLIND SIDE
FAVORITE ICE CREAM 	CHOCOLATE CHERRY CHIP
HOBBIES	TAKING PICTURES, FCA, AND BAKING
RANDOM FACT	TOOK TRICK RIDING LESSONS WHEN YOUNGER

ENCOURAGE MORE, CRITICIZE LESS

Volleyball is a game where points happen quickly. When you are competitive and want to win, it is easy to become frustrated. Either your team does something good and you get a point, or someone on your team makes a mistake and you lose the point. That means there are a lot of opportunities to get frustrated with yourself or your teammates.

When I played high school club volleyball, I learned I had two options. I could get mad that a teammate had lost a point. But I quickly learned it did not help my team. It brought me down and my teammates down, and I was not being the light of Christ to those around me. In those situations I let my emotions take control. However, there was another option; to take the opportunity to build others up.

No one likes making a mistake or letting their team down. Hearing an encouraging word can give confidence. During my freshman year of college, I got to put this into action. I redshirted and the only way I had a part in games was with the words I shouted from the sideline. God humbled me and taught me that it can be just as rewarding to encourage teammates when it was the only way you can contribute in games.

However, God never promised that being a Christian would be easy. Halfway through my senior season of college volleyball, a freshman took my starting spot. I struggled and it was tough at times to not let bitterness or mean remarks get in the way. But that is not what God wanted. As Christians, God trusts us to go out and be a light for Him. There is no better way to do that than by encouraging our teammates. Whether it is on or off the court, as a freshman or a senior, for your best friend or someone you barely know, everyone is on the same team. Your purpose is to be a light for Christ. One kind word, one encouraging cheer can make a difference, not only in your teammate's play, but also in their view of Christ.

1. *The next time you are frustrated with a teammate, what is a verse or prayer you can memorize to think about to help you build them up instead of bring them down?*

"Do not let any unwholesome talk come out of your mouths, but only what is helpful for building others up according to their needs, that it may benefit those who listen."
Ephesians 4:29 (NIV)

08

ANDREW MOMENT

TENNIS

UNIVERSITY	JUDSON UNIVERSITY
HOMETOWN	YORKVILLE, ILLINOIS
JERSEY	N/A
POSITION	N/A
FAVORITE ATHLETE	RODGER FEDERER AND PETE SAMPRAS
FAVORITE MOVIE	PLANET OF THE APES
FAVORITE ICE CREAM	MINT CHOCOLATE
HOBBIES	GUITAR, PING PONG, FISHING
RANDOM FACT	RAN FIRST 5K AT AGE 20

BETTER THAN BITTER

When I pray, I am constantly asking God for forgiveness, begging Him to show me the grace and mercy needed to still love me despite the fact that I continually sin against Him. I know many of you reading this right now can relate and we all tend to take more than we give as far as grace goes. Do not interpret this as saying that we should not ask for forgiveness, for it is definitely necessary. But instead of merely asking for it, how much different would things be if we also started showing that type of forgiveness to others?

I recall a time when I was so bitter towards someone that I honestly hoped that I would never see them again. I literally prayed that God would remove that person from my life for good. I called my mom, assuming that she would take my side because, well, that is what moms do. But she ended up telling me that I should forgive this person, and I learned a valuable lesson that day; being affronted and offended is always a choice.

We choose to be upset because we feel that we have been wronged and are owed something, be it an apology or worldly material. Sure, that person may have hurt us, but he is accountable only to God. He commands us to forgive and to shy away from harboring bitterness. I have heard a lack of forgiveness explained this way: "You wouldn't drink poison and wait for the other person to die, would you? That's pretty much what you're doing when you hold a grudge."

Through Jesus Christ, we are offered true freedom. I can tell you first–hand that living with anger and bitterness is not living the free life. It is a dark path that is traveled so easily and so often. We are promised freedom through Christ. By choosing to forgive transgressions and give up being offended, we are obeying God and saying yes, His will, His wants, and His ways.

1. *What do you need to do in order to make things right with someone who has wronged you?*

"See to it that no one falls short of the grace of God and that no bitter root grows up to cause trouble and defile many."

Hebrews 12:15 (NIV)

09

ANDREW CORDASCO

FOOTBALL

UNIVERSITY	LIBERTY UNIVERSITY
HOMETOWN	WILLIAMSBURG, VIRGINIA
JERSEY	#88
POSITION	TIGHT END
FAVORITE ATHLETE	HEATH MILLER
FAVORITE MOVIE	LORD OF THE RINGS TRILOGY
FAVORITE ICE CREAM	MOOSE TRACKS
HOBBIES	GUITAR, DRUMS, FISHING, HIKING
RANDOM FACT	GAINED 40 POUNDS FIRST YEAR OF COLLEGE

THE COST OF INDIFFERENCE

Lukewarm is neither hot nor cold; it essentially means to just be stuck in the middle. No one wants to ice an injury with this kind of water. No, you need it cold! Who wants to shower in lukewarm water? Fat chance!

Sometimes, as an athlete, it becomes so easy to just coast and become lukewarm; through a workout, a practice, and even sometimes a game or competition if the contest is no longer competitive.

I used to get so exhausted in the weight room that it would be so tempting to just skip that last rep of pull ups or slack off during two-a-days when heads were turned away. I have been incredibly indifferent. Don't get me wrong, I have a passion for the game and I would not have traded those opportunities, but when something is challenging, it takes a highly disciplined soul to keep the foot on the gas all of the time.

In 1 Corinthians 9:24, Paul lays it all out for us. We are to run the race in such a way that we might, you know, win! Whatever your sport, you are competing against someone else, whether it be your teammate, an opponent, or a starting position.

How does this translate for us spiritually? In Revelation 3:16 God tells us that the half-hearted Christians will literally be spit out of His mouth. He wants believers who are on fire for Him! So often as Christians it becomes easy to become comfortable and coast through our walk with God and check a list: "Okay I read my Bible, I'm good", or, "Well, I go to church so that's good!" When we finally begin to seek Him, to crave His word, to let Him guide us in life, we too can be on fire for the Lord, and that's exactly where I want to be! What about you?

1. *What are some ways that I can alter my perspective and "run to win" on a daily basis?*

"Do you not know that in a race all the runner run, but only one gets the prize? Run in such a way as to get the prize."

1 Corinthians 9:24 (NIV)

10

ALLIE NEWSOM

SOCCER

UNIVERSITY	ILLINOIS STATE UNIVERSITY
HOMETOWN	MANTENO, ILLINOIS
JERSEY	#27
POSITION	DEFENSIVE MIDFIELDER
FAVORITE ATHLETE	KURT WARNER
FAVORITE MOVIE	ARGO
FAVORITE ICE CREAM	COOKIE DOUGH
HOBBIES	COFFEE SHOPS, THE INTERNET, ORGANIZING
RANDOM FACT	IDENTICAL TWIN WHO ALSO PLAYS AT ILLINOIS

GAINING BY GIVING

Ever since I can remember, I have hated running. Yet I chose a sport where nothing happens...without running.

I am neither fast, nor quick. But in high school, technical skill and clever play masked that deficiency. The decision to play Division I soccer brought with it the realization that my battle with running was far from over.

I will never forget that day. My first running packet had just arrived in the mail and I began to envision what I was in for that summer. In addition to all of the drills that I was required to complete, the packet contained a detailed description of the fitness test that all players must pass on the first day of preseason camp. The packet, it seemed, demanded the impossible; it was nothing but a physical representation of my weaknesses and future failures. Summer vacation soon became an agonizing time of anxiety, a fearing of the unknown: Would I pass? Would all of my work pay off?

The fitness test soon became my sole focus before every preseason since. I would evaluate how well the beginning of my season was going by how well I did on the fitness test. It wasn't until my senior year that I realized I had been setting myself up for failure all along. We are all control freaks, but it is magnified and reveals itself more intensely in the realm of sports. I had been holding on so tightly to my performance each year that I didn't leave any room for God to work.

When we try to control things on our own, we actually end up with less of it. But when we give up control and surrender it all to Jesus, we gain the stability we seek. It is then that we will truly experience the peace and tranquility that we were always meant to have.

1. *In what parts of your athletic life are you clinging to, refusing to let go and let God take over?*

"For whoever wants to save their life will lose it, but whoever loses their life for me will find it."

Mathew 16:25 (NIV)

11

ANDREW NEWLIN

BASEBALL

UNIVERSITY 	ANDERSON UNIVERSITY
HOMETOWN 	WICHITA, KANSAS
JERSEY	#12
POSITION	FIRST BASE
FAVORITE ATHLETE 	JOSH HAMILTON AND JOSE REYES
FAVORITE MOVIE 	THE SANDLOT
FAVORITE ICE CREAM 	HOMEMADE VANILLA
HOBBIES 	DISC GOLF, LONGBOARDING
RANDOM FACT 	HASN'T BEEN TO THE EMERGENCY ROOM YET

PINCHING PRIDE

By the numbers, my sophomore year was my best one. I sported a .431 batting average and committed very few errors at first base. By the same token, the numbers also show that my junior year was the exact opposite. I had more strikeouts than hits and before long I had player after player walking up to me in the batting cage trying to tell me the best solution for my poor performance.

When I compare my spiritual walk with the Lord to my baseball career in high school, noticeable parallels emerge. When I was successful on the baseball diamond, pride flooded my life and my relationship with the Lord suffered. But when I struggled, I was humbled and my relationship with the Him strengthened.

If pride was water, my life was a boat with a hole in the bottom. I was always scooping it out of the boat, but no matter how hard I tried, pride always seeped back in. It took me seventeen years to realize that fighting pride isn't the solution. Although we must wake up every day ready to go to war against the sins in our life, battling pride does not lead to long–term change; it is only a momentary fix. In order to discover long–lasting victory over pride, we must replace pride with humility. We should all strive to live by Philippians 2:3-4: "Do nothing out of selfish ambition or vain conceit. Rather, in humility value others above yourselves, not looking to your own interests but each of you to the interests of the others."

1. *What are some ways that you can replace price with humility?*

"But he gives us more grace. That is why Scripture says: God opposes the proud but shows favor to the humble."
James 4:6 (NIV)

12

BRAXTON TUCKER

BASKETBALL

UNIVERSITY	UNIVERSITY OF MARY HARDIN-BAYLOR
HOMETOWN	SALADO, TEXAS
JERSEY	#20
POSITION	FORWARD
FAVORITE ATHLETE	KEVIN DURANT AND DWIGHT HOWARD
FAVORITE MOVIE	FOREST GUMP
FAVORITE ICE CREAM	COOKIES 'N CREAM
HOBBIES	GOLF, PING PONG, LONGBOARDING, GUITAR
RANDOM FACT	SLEEPWALKED ON A CRUISE SHIP

TRANSFORMING YOUR GAME

After redshirting my first year in college, I spent the summer training and getting excited for the upcoming season. One of the first games was a trip to Washington. During the preseason, I ultimately surprised my coaches and teammates.

Shortly after, right before the preseason games, I dealt with a couple of injuries. I was not going to be able to make the trip that I had been working toward. I was extremely discouraged and was questioning God through all of this.

After missing all of preseason and a fair share of early games, I battled through practice with a cast on for two weeks. During this time, we lost three guys due to injuries. I played a couple of minutes here and there, not having a lot of opportunity to shine. As we moved into the playoffs, I accepted my role on the team and trusted God to use me in His perfect time.

We lost the conference tournament, got into the NCAA tournament and continued to advance game by game. I ended up traveling to Washington one weekend and Virginia the next. We ended up in the 2013 DIII National Championship for the 75th anniversary and played in Atlanta Georgia at Philips Arena along with the DI Final Four next door in the Georgia Dome.

When I think of transformation, I think of change for the better. God gives us many blessings and opportunities in life. Many times we want things to go our way. When I was questioning God's plan for me, I definitely thought I knew what was best for me. The Lord completely transformed how I thought "my" season should have been for His plans. Just as the Lord can transform our plans, he ultimately transforms who we are and who we were created to be in Him. Transformation begins when we stop comparing ourselves to teammates and when we live for Christ who gave His life for us so that we could live to the fullest.

This verse reminds me that transformation occurs when we renew our minds daily with who Christ is and who we are in Him. God's will is good, acceptable and perfect. I am confident the Lord has plans for you. When you allow him to use your talents in your "transformed state," you will begin to make an impact on those around you. You will begin living as a new creation knowing God's will for your life will always be what is best even if it seems tough.

1. *What are some ways that you can replace pride with humility?*

"Do not conform to the pattern of this world, but be transformed by the renewing of your mind. Then you will be able to test and approve what God's will is–his good, pleasing and perfect will."

Romans 12:2 (NIV)

13

BRAD SMITH

FOOTBALL

UNIVERSITY — UNIVERSITY OF MISSOURI

HOMETOWN  — YOUNGSTOWN, OHIO

JERSEY  — #16

POSITION 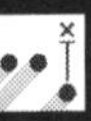 — QUARTERBACK

FAVORITE ATHLETE  — RANDALL CUNNINGHAM

FAVORITE MOVIE — I SPY (EDDIE MURPHY AND OWEN WILSON)

FAVORITE ICE CREAM  — BUTTER PECAN

HOBBIES  — LOVES TO DESIGN, AND GO FISHING

RANDOM FACT  — DRAFTED:2006, ROUND 4, PICK 7

REMEMBER ME NOT

Athletics are based on repetition. From fundamentals, to play, to pregame rituals, continuity is ever present. The questions posed to athletes are no different. No matter the level, whether high school, college, or the pros, everybody always seems to talk about one thing: Legacy. What will you leave behind? How do you want to be remembered?

My answer to this question is quite simple: don't remember me at all. Not for the things I've done at the University of Missouri or in the NFL—none of it. The only way that stuff will ever matter is if it brought God's glory on the field. I do not need to be remembered to validate my existence. God has already done that by sending his only Son to die not only for me, but for every single one of us. I do not need folks to reminisce on the most successful moments of my career because God has deemed it unnecessary. The only thing that needs to be remembered is what I did for Jesus.

So remember Jesus instead. He's the one who deserves it. He, above all others, should be afforded the highest praise and honor that comes with remembering those who have passed on. For all of the aspiring athletes reading this right now, here's a bit of advice for you: Realize your inadequacies. Humble yourself and admit that you do not have it all together. Be a witness to others, even amidst persecution. This is what makes faith hard, but it's also what makes God worth it. Trust in the Scripture. Trust in the good news of the Gospel because to do so is to trust Him. Always remember that when you feel the urge, as we all do, to focus on your own selfish needs, turn the attention to Him instead. Remember Him, not me.

1. *What can you do to further His kingdom, and bring more of his children back home to Him?*

"Why, you do not even know what will happen tomorrow. What is your life? You are a mist that appears for a little while and then vanishes."
James 4:14 (NIV)

14

KATIE RUSSO

CROSS-COUNTRY - TRACK

UNIVERSITY	LIBERTY UNIVERSITY
HOMETOWN	FORT MYERS, FLORIDA
JERSEY	N/A
POSITION	N/A
FAVORITE ATHLETE	RYAN HALL
FAVORITE MOVIE	PRIDE AND PREJUDICE
FAVORITE ICE CREAM	MINT CHIP
HOBBIES	PADDLE BOARDING, PAINTING, READING
RANDOM FACT	SWAM WITH BELUGA WHALES

POUR IT ALL OUT

The phrase "finishing the race" is a simple, logical one that is not always easy to accomplish. As a runner, this command means a lot to me, but it can be applied to many different facets of life.

Not only does it literally relate to finishing a physical race, more importantly, it symbolically represents finishing the race of life. With every completed season, there must be a start. It is at the start where I have learned to strive for excellence and to be adamantly determined to finish, accepting what God already has in store no matter what I may gain.

When I start a cross-country or track race, the pain I endure is a form of sacrifice. God is pleased with our sacrifices, which ultimately brings Him glory through our talent. When Paul talks specifically about being a "drink offering," this kind of sacrifice requires a complete surrender of potential, personal benefit for the one sacrificing. It is giving without any strings attached.

Unfortunately, injuries are a common occurrence that athletes must face. Having had my share of injuries, I know how it feels to be discouraged. I always want to give my best. Yet, in the midst of struggle, God reminds me of my commitment to continue pressing toward the finish line, which forces me to put my prideful focus on success aside. I have learned that by deciding to give it my all, even if it means that I do not get the results I think I deserve, God's faithfulness is illuminated, causing pride to slowly fade away.

Following Jesus does not always mean that we will get the earthly reward we desire. But, it does mean that His plan will be accomplished. In the end, God will have His way and this truth is one of the best training tools and biggest confidence boosters I have truly come to embrace. As an athlete, I challenge you to lay your talent and season on the altar as a "drink offering" knowing that these things are a blessing from the Lord.

1. *What are some specific things that you need to "pour out on the altar" as a sacrifice to the Lord?*

"For I am already being poured out like a drink offering, and the time for my departure is near. I have fought the good fight, I have finished the race, I have kept the faith."

2 Timothy 4:6-7 (NIV)

15

GIGI MEYER

VOLLEYBALL

UNIVERSITY	FLORIDA GULF COAST UNIVERSITY
HOMETOWN	GAINESVILLE, FLORIDA
JERSEY	#5
POSITION	SETTER
FAVORITE ATHLETE	TIM TEBOW
FAVORITE MOVIE	FINDING NEMO
FAVORITE ICE CREAM	COFFEE FLAVORED
HOBBIES	WAKEBOARDING, MOVIES, COOKING
RANDOM FACT	3 FEARS: SPIDERS, SMALL SPACES, VAMPIRES

BETTER THAN LOMBARDI

Anyone who has ever seriously invested in playing organized sports knows that good coaching is crucial to maximizing your potential. Without it, we simply would not know what to do or how to do it. I have been blessed with many a great coach during my career, but none greater than God. He coaches me not only on the court, but in every aspect off of it too from athletics to academics, from relationships to friendships. He's taught me lessons throughout my life that no one else could ever teach me, because He knows me better than anyone else, even myself.

If I did not have this type of relationship with God, sports would definitely be a lot more difficult to take part in, for he reminds me to put others before myself and to stay composed when under pressure. I doubt that I would be a good role model if He was not the biggest part of my life; He calms me when the chaos comes calling.

One such instance of this chaos happened when I fractured a vertebrae in a wakeboarding accident. I was put out of commission for two months. Even after that I had to ease back into things. This transition hit me pretty hard and I experienced a short depression period, one where I failed to pursue Christ for comfort and strength. But when I came to my senses, and thus God, I was able to cope and wade through the choppy waters, back to calming currents. Calming amidst the chaos.

When all of the calm and chaos has ceased and I am with my Lord and Savior up in Heaven, I want people to remember me as a steady, selfless, and genuine human being. Someone who loved and cared for everyone, and was always a positive influence on those around her. Someone who truly lived to bring God glory and portrayed the love that He calls of everyone. Someone who was not only a player coached by God, but also a servant of Him as well.

1. *How can you let God coach your life?*

"I am the vine; you are the branches. If you remain in me and I in you, you will bear much fruit; apart from me you can do nothing."

John 15:5 (NIV)

16

DAVID BACKES

HOCKEY

UNIVERSITY  MINNESOTA STATE UNIVERSITY

HOMETOWN  BLAINE, MINNESOTA

JERSEY #42

POSITION  CENTER, SHOOTS RIGHT

FAVORITE ATHLETE  WAYNE GRETZKY

FAVORITE MOVIE  ROCKY

FAVORITE ICE CREAM  CARAMEL COLLISION

HOBBIES  FLYING PLANES AND SHOOTING GUNS

RANDOM FACT FOUNDED ATHLETES FOR ANIMALS IN 2013

THE ONE WAY WE RISE

Everybody knows that as Christians, we must have one focus: serving and loving God. When attempting to do this, trying to be holy men and women of God, sometimes it is easy to put forth all of our energies into reading the Word, praying to Him and cultivating a relationship with our Lord and Savior Jesus Christ.

While all of these things are of the utmost importance and are required of a good Christian, we often forget about those around us. We often forget about His flock, about God's children. We are called not only to love God, but His people as well. Loving His children and building community with them is also, by extension, loving Him.

It is not only important to devote time to nurturing and caring for God's people, but it also aids you in your own walk with God. A good support system is necessary and the attributes of these folks are contagious. Good Christians rub off on you. If you surround yourself with Godly people, you will blossom and doing the right thing will not only become easier, it will become second–nature and a huge part of your lifestyle.

The only way to grow is together. Everyone has innate social needs. Why? Why would God bestow us with such traits? So that we would seek out each other's company. So that we may support each other through life's trials. So that we may all lift each other up when we are weary from our journey to Him. So that we may draw God's strength through our fellow children that He created.

Our God is a giver of gifts. No matter where you look you can see them. Oxygen via plants. Food via animals. And love via his brothers and sisters in Him. This love is right there for us, available wherever His children reside. All we have to do is accept it.

1. *What can you do to share God's love with his children and build community?*

"For where two or three gather in my name, there am I with them."
Mathew 18:20 (NIV)

17

DAN CASEY

FOOTBALL

UNIVERSITY	DAVIDSON COLLEGE
HOMETOWN	TEGA CAY, SOUTH CAROLINA
JERSEY	#9
POSITION	SAFETY
FAVORITE ATHLETE	ERIC LIDDELL
FAVORITE MOVIE	A RIVER RUNS THROUGHT IT
FAVORITE ICE CREAM	MINT CHOCOLATE CHIP
HOBBIES	THE GREAT OUTDOORS-ALL OF IT
RANDOM FACT	HAS 11 SIBLINGS

PURELY HIS

Purity. Most people squirm when they hear this word. Maybe you think you're doing pretty well, but maybe, quite possibly, your view of the concept is tainted. While Christians regard it as one of the most important commandments, our culture makes light of it. We are under so much pressure to conform to the world and pressure to live out our faith.

The truth is, neither of these stances is correct. Maybe you are still going strong, saving yourself for marriage, or perhaps you've stumbled countless times along the way; but no matter where you stand today, you are not pure on your own. You are marred by your own sinful nature.

But before you hang your head, remember this: The blood of Jesus Christ has cleansed you, and washed away your sins. You are not pure because of what you do. You are not pure because you have the self-control to abstain. It is only because of Christ, and what He did for you, that you are pure.

Knowing where your purity came from should not be used as a "get out of jail free" card. We should instead live in gratitude for the grace He has given us, for it is a gift. Accept it today and rejoice in Him.

1. Are you pure of heart? Do your thoughts and actions reflect that answer?

"So if the Son sets you free, you will be free indeed."
John 8:36 (NIV)

18

CHRIS FIELDS

TENNIS

UNIVERSITY		UNIVERSITY OF ARKANSAS
HOMETOWN		KANSAS CITY, KANSAS
JERSEY		N/A
POSITION		N/A
FAVORITE ATHLETE		ROGER FEDERER
FAVORITE MOVIE		THE LION KING
FAVORITE ICE CREAM		STRAWBERRY
HOBBIES		GUITAR AND THE OUTDOORS
RANDOM FACT		HAS LIVED IN SWITZERLAND

IDENTITY IN CHRIST

Life is not easy. Every one of us has experienced the world trying to bring us down at some point. The sports world, like the real world, is full of naysayers and people who want you to fail. Growing up, I loved sports: soccer, tennis, running. Eventually, I decided tennis was my true passion and I dedicated more time to it. This decision was a very interesting one and was met with a lot of skepticism. Most of it stemmed from the fact that I have been missing my right hand since birth.

Over the years, I had coaches tell me that there was a certain level I could not achieve, and there were certain shots I could never hit. At a young age, my left hand wasn't strong enough for a one-handed backhand. When things got rough and it seemed like the obstacles were too much to overcome, I remembered Psalm 27. In this passage, David showed me that if your faith and identity are in Christ, you have nothing to fear from the world's so-called insurmountable challenges. Thanks to the hope Scripture provided and other coaches who encouraged me, I achieved what the others said was impossible.

Since then, I have found that God has equipped each and every one of us for His plan. Our differences are what make us special. Although the world may say we are inadequate, God specifically tailored us for His purpose and no one can do your part better than you. We are a part of God's plan on this earth, and He commands us to spread His hope, love and encouragement to those around us. You never know the impact that one uplifting word could have on a teammate's life. Now, every time I travel for tennis I am reminded that through God all things are possible, Every time I step out on the court, I cannot help but feel a deep sense of gratitude for those who stuck with me and personified Hebrews 10:24. "If the Lord is your fortress then nothing can overcome you. Through the power of the Lord, you can overcome anything."

1. What are some of the challenges in your life that you need to fully give to God?

"The LORD is my light and my salvation–whom shall I fear? The LORD is the stronghold of my life–of whom shall I be afraid? When the wicked advance against me to devour me, it is my enemies and my foes who will stumble and fall. Though an army besiege me, my heart will not fear; though war break out against me, even then I will be confident."
Psalm 27:1-3 (NIV)

19

CAROLINE STANLEY

SOCCER

UNIVERSITY	UNIVERSITY OF SOUTHERN CALIFORNIA
HOMETOWN	LEE'S SUMMIT, MISSOURI
JERSEY	#12
POSITION	GOAL KEEPER
FAVORITE ATHLETE	KEVIN DURANT
FAVORITE MOVIE	THE NOTEBOOK
FAVORITE ICE CREAM	CHOCOLATE PEANUT BUTTER
HOBBIES	WRITING, PADDLE BOARDING, COFFEE SHOPS
RANDOM FACT	SHE LOVES SNOW

IT'S OKAY THAT YOU'RE NOT OKAY

You fake a smile. You force some laughter. You tell someone that your day has been "good" and wince a bit inside as the words escape your lips. We have all felt like this at some point in our lives. Whether it has lasted a day, a week, or a lifetime, everyone has been "not okay" before.

I was not always backing up Hope Solo. But, I have always been two things: a tomboy and good at soccer. I was bullied a lot in school for my tomboyishness. Because of soccer, I did not really have a normal homecoming, prom, party, and high school experience. I felt lonely and alienated.

I left for the University of Missouri, ready to start a new chapter in my life. I had just won nationals and I was the #1 ranked goalie in the country. I was on cloud nine, but something was still amiss. Then things started to spiral.

I was dumped twice, by my boyfriend and by the university. After that, I didn't want to go to class. I didn't want to work out. I didn't even want to play soccer. I just sat in my dorm room, until one day my roommate pulled me back to reality. We went and kicked soccer balls until I cried and boxed until I broke down. I even cried in church the next day, a first for me.

During my sophomore year, after I transferred to the University of Southern California, God entered my life. I will never forget the sermon that He spoke through the preacher. He said that we are all masterpieces and we are the children of the most unbelievable artist. Little did I know, but that was a blanket of mercy covering and protecting me all along. I began to realize that we do not have to have it all together. We cannot be perfect people. But God's love is unconditional. No matter how many times we turn our backs on Him, He will never do that to us. We may make mistakes, but He does not. He will love us even if we get dumped by others. You are no exception.

1. Is it hard for you to accept that you're not okay?

"You will again have compassion on us; you will tread our sins underfoot and hurl all our iniquities into the depths of the sea."

Micah 7:19 (NIV)

20

ABBY HAWLEY

SOFTBALL

UNIVERSITY		MINNESOTA STATE UNIVERSITY
HOMETOWN		URBANDALE, IOWA
JERSEY		#16
POSITION	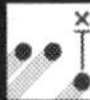	SECOND BASE
FAVORITE ATHLETE		KURT WARNER AND JENNIE FINCH
FAVORITE MOVIE		SISTER ACT 2 AND A LEAGUE OF THEIR OWN
FAVORITE ICE CREAM		VANILLA BEAN AND COOKIE DOUGH
HOBBIES		HANGING OUT WITH FAMILY
RANDOM FACT		BORN ON A LEAP YEAR

GENTLY MEEK

When I used to hear the word meek, I would instinctively correlate it with the word weak. I wasn't trying to jump–start my rap career, but the definition of those two words are very similar, yet so incredibly different.

Athletes are generally associated with strength, both of the mental and physical variety. The Lord instilled both talent and a competitive nature in every athlete, qualities that we are able to utilize on fields, courts, and tracks. Or the diamond, in my case, for 17 years of my life. Pair that with the public accolades, admirable statistics, and constant recognition that were regular staples of my playing days. One can see how an athlete may develop a prideful nature.

Paul, a man shackled in chains, challenged believers to live their lives in a manner that was worthy of a higher calling. He asserted that being meek and gentle were two ways of doing this. Meekness as opposed to pride, for it is a humble attitude directly related to the nature of our heart. In my mind it seemed so wimpy, far from the view of what a worldly athlete should look like. In actuality, displaying meekness is a sign of great fortitude and courage, for it symbolizes our submission to Christ and our service towards others, both on and off the playing field.

Meekness is refraining from retaliating against an opponent who is purposely trying to get a rise out of you. It's not beaning the opposing pitcher when she comes up to the plate, even though she did so intentionally earlier in the game. It is laying down your pride, and mustering the discipline to do what pleases Him instead.

When a teammate wrongs you, gentleness means forgiving their actions and moving forward rather than seeking revenge. When a coach sits you on the bench for no apparent reason, it means continually serving him or her by working hard at practice. As believers, we must pursue gentleness and wear it like a garment. We may be ridiculed on earth, but in Heaven, I assure you that we will be applauded and praised.

1. What prevents you from having a gentle and meek heart towards those around you?

"Therefore as God's chosen people, holy and dearly loved, clothe yourselves with compassion, kindness, humility, gentleness and patience. Bear with each other and forgive one another if any of you has a grievance against someone. Forgive as the LORD forgave you."

Colossians 3:12-13 (NIV)

21

DAN HAGAMAN

FOOTBALL

UNIVERSITY		VANDERBILT UNIVERSITY
HOMETOWN		NASHVILLE, TENNESSEE
JERSEY		#84
POSITION		RECEIVER
FAVORITE ATHLETE		WES WELKER
FAVORITE MOVIE		STAR WARS
FAVORITE ICE CREAM		MINT CHOCOLATE CHIP
HOBBIES		BACKPACKING, FISHING
RANDOM FACT		HAS A DEATHLY FEAR OF SHARKS

WORRYING: WASTED ENERGY

Life as a student athlete can be a stressful one. From practice, to workouts, to class, there are few free moments during the week. As a football player at Vanderbilt University, I had ambitions to go to medical school and become a doctor. My freshman year, I seriously underestimated how difficult it would be to balance the commitment of SEC football with rigorous Vanderbilt "pre-med" academics. Before long, I was extremely stressed out and worry began to take over my life. The more I let worry creep into my life, the more my performance suffered both on the field and in the classroom. Next thing I knew, I was dropping balls during practice and making poor grades on my chemistry and biology tests. I knew something had to change.

During my early years at Vanderbilt, I had put the pursuit of success before my pursuit of God. Everything I did was working toward my own personal gain and achievement. I needed to seriously reevaluate my priorities. The more I tried to pursue goals only for personal gain, the more I worried about falling short of those goals. I realized that God has the ultimate plan for my life and worry is nothing more than a waste of energy.

Proverbs 25:29 reads, "The fear of man brings a snare, but whoever trusts in the LORD shall be safe." At the end of the day, God holds the ultimate plan for each and every one of our lives. When we worry, we are doubting His plan and trying take control into our own hands.

Moving forward, I am working hard to put God first in all areas of my life. The Bible repeatedly tells us to cast away all anxieties and pursue what is truly important. We will never be able to "worry away our problems" so why do we waste so much energy trying to do so? Instead of worrying over earthy pursuits, we are called to rest in peace knowing that the almighty God has a plan for our lives that is bigger than we can imagine.

1. What are some specific tests or trials in your current life that are causing you to worry?

"Can any one of you by worrying add a single hour to your life?"
Matthew 6:27 (NIV)

22

GABRIELLE CLARK

BASKETBALL

UNIVERSITY	SAN DIEGO STATE UNIVERSITY
HOMETOWN	LOS ANGELOS, CALIFORNIA
JERSEY	#22
POSITION	FORWARD
FAVORITE ATHLETE	MAYA MOORE AND KEVIN DURANT
FAVORITE MOVIE	A WALK TO REMEMBER
FAVORITE ICE CREAM	COOKIES 'N CREAM
HOBBIES	PLAYING WITH KIDS AND BAKING
RANDOM FACT	CLEANS WHEN BORED

WHO ARE YOU PLAYING FOR?

Before I fully understood what it meant to play my sport for God, my audience of one, I looked to others for approval and praise. I lacked confidence, which hindered my performance, because I was looking to family, teammates, coaches, friends, and fans for their acceptance. My game was focused on constantly seeking to satisfy and please humans. I was practicing and competing everyday for the wrong audience. Since I was seeking to please humanity instead of the Lord, I put my athletic ability and skills in a box because of my fear of making mistakes and not being accepted.

It was the summer before my senior year that I fully allowed God to be on the court with me. He transformed my mind and performance. Competing with God as my sole audience made me turn away from others for their acceptance. I now understood that whether I had the best game of my career or the worst game, I was accepted and worthy of God's love. Competing for humans only gave me temporary satisfaction, but competing for God gave me truth and the promises that I am always accepted, worthy, protected, and lack nothing.

Entering my senior year, I was confident and excited to play knowing that God saw me as perfect in all situations. Competing with the truths that He declared about me gave me joy, comfort, and strength on the court. Christ delivered me from the bondage of insecurity, which once held me back from showcasing the athletic ability and skills He blessed me with. My senior year was my best and most enjoyable collegiate season because I stopped competing for everyone and began competing for the Lord.

1. How can your sport and performance be transformed when you compete for your audience of one?

"Whatever you do, work at it with all your heart, as working for the Lord, not for human masters"

Colossians 3:23 (NIV)

23

KRISTIN MORRISON

CROSS-COUNTRY - TRACK

UNIVERSITY UNIVERSITY OF ILLINOIS ALUMNUS

HOMETOWN BOLINGBROOK, ILLINOIS

JERSEY N/A

POSITION EVENT: HEPTATHLON

FAVORITE ATHLETE CHUCK NORRIS AND JACKIE JOYNER-KERSEE

FAVORITE MOVIE PRIDE AND PREJUDICE AND WARRIOR

FAVORITE ICE CREAM BIRTHDAY CAKE

HOBBIES PAINTING, SINGING, GUITAR, CROSSFIT

RANDOM FACT ENJOYS CHRISTMAS AND DISNEY MUSIC

THE WILL OF WORDS

Our chant from the beginning of the year was "BTC!" which stands for "Big Ten Champions." It was my senior year and we all knew something was different, something was special. We had a fire that could not be stifled. We were one in likeness of mind and the certainty of our hearts was in our cry of "BTC!" We were not getting bamboozled for second place again.

The night before the three day competition for the Indoor Big Ten Championships began, our coaches told us that if everything went as they had planned, we could take first place by a couple points or so. They left the room to give us time to prepare. I do not know what took over me at that moment, but I'm glad it did. I stood up and reminded my teammates that I was going to give my all for Christ and the rest for them. I also promised them I would set some personal records and score a point for the team.

At this time, I had competed in the heptathlon (seven events scored as one) for only three years. Other girls had practiced for at least a decade. I had never scored in the Big Ten, let alone made it in the top ten finishes.

The next morning, I woke up and competed. I faced some adversity, but my words and heart remained true. I wanted to score one point for my God and my team. I cannot explain how I did some things that day, but I do have four personal records out of five events from that competition. And my team won by several points–we did what we said we would.

As a team, we spoke about life and success to each other and we left no room for fear or failure. I continuously quoted scripture over myself and my teammates. I knew God gave me life, power and peace for everything, so why would not His word do the same?

Commit His words to heart. Speak life, love and truth to one another. I guarantee you will be amazed at what God can do.

1. How can you speak life and truth into your team and coaches on and off the competition field?

"The tongue has the power of life and death, and those who love it will eat its fruit."
Proverbs 18:21 (NIV)

24

ANGEL MAGNO

LACROSSE

UNIVERSITY	JAMES MADISON UNIVERSITY
HOMETOWN	GAITHERSBURG, MARYLAND
JERSEY	#15
POSITION	ATTACK
FAVORITE ATHLETE	ROBERT GRIFFIN III AND GABBY DOUGLAS
FAVORITE MOVIE	HARRY POTTER SERIES
FAVORITE ICE CREAM	BUTTERFINGER
HOBBIES	NAPPING, EATING, PLAYING WITH PUPPIES
RANDOM FACT	SAYS "HICCUP" WHEN SHE HICCUPS

GIFTS FROM A LOVING FATHER

Junior year of high school brought with it a very exciting time of my life; the recruiting process. I was all set to play college lacrosse until my senior year. That's when I tore my ACL, PCL, and meniscus while tumbling during a cheerleading practice. I was forced to wait 3 months for surgery, by which time most of my college offers had been rescinded.

Everything was going swimmingly up until that point and I was constantly thanking God. But then my world was completely flipped upside down. I slipped into a mild depression and feared that my playing days were over. The depression spiraled and I became so angry with God that I stopped praying and started complaining instead. "Why me?" How could you let this happen now?" I kept focusing on the one setback, yet ignoring the friends and family constantly supporting me; major proof of God's blessings in my life.

I ended up attending (and loving) James Madison University and joining their club lacrosse team. It wasn't until I finished my sophomore year that I realized what God had planned for me all along. I love my team, I couldn't have asked for a better group of girls to become my sisters. The program is still very competitive and I get plenty of playing time. We even went to Colorado for the National Championships! He ended up delivering me happiness in the end. I see now that God took away lacrosse for a while because I had made it an idol. I won't lie, I worshiped my sport and would have done anything to play college ball.

From this experience, I've learned that throughout all the good times and all the bad times you have to continually look to God and never lose faith. I would not be where I am today, playing for the team that I love or studying at my dream school, if I had things my way. We must always remember to give thanks in all things not just for all things.

1. Is there anything keeping you from fully focusing on God?

"Rejoice always, pray continually, give thanks in all circumstances; for this is God's will for you in Christ Jesus."

1 Thessalonians 5:16-18 (NIV)

25

EDDIE ABOUSSIE

FOOTBALL

UNIVERSITY		UNIVERSITY OF TEXAS
HOMETOWN		WICHITA FALLS, TEXAS
JERSEY		#44
POSITION		RUNNING BACK
FAVORITE ATHLETE		JOEY ABOUSSIE
FAVORITE MOVIE		GLADIATOR
FAVORITE ICE CREAM		ROCKY ROAD
HOBBIES		GUITAR AND SINGING
RANDOM FACT		IS LEBANESE

SEEK HIS FAVOR

I was blessed to play football at the University of Texas. When I read the verse below it takes me back to Spring Ball and Fall Camp my senior year. Every practice, I had one goal in mind, to please my position coach. I wanted almost nothing more than to do good in his eyes, so he would play me during my last year of football. I was not the starter or even the back-up, but that did not stop me from working my hardest to get in a game. My coach was fair and I got a lot of looks in practices and scrimmages leading up to my senior year. Almost every play, no matter if it was good or bad, I would catch myself looking at my coach to see if he would give me praise or scold me. I caught myself seeking the favor of a man instead of trying to please God.

During a scrimmage at the end of Fall Camp, I screwed up my right knee during a play and had surgery, which ended my dream of playing in a game my senior year. God really showed me how quickly dreams of self-glory can be taken away. He truly does not care how many yards you get in a game or if you even get to play in a game. No matter what level of athletics you play, there is something intoxicating when you make a big play and you gain approval in the eyes of the fans, your coaches and your teammates. Humans, especially athletes, are inclined to seek affirmation and glory from others.

To be a follower of Christ means you have actively chosen a lifestyle to serve Him alone. That does not mean stop playing sports, but your natural talents, whatever they may be, were given to you by God to serve and glorify Him.

The end of Galatians 1:10 states "If I were still trying to please men, I would not be a bondservant of Christ." This shows that you cannot try to please men and God. You can either put your efforts in men who may or may not accept you; or as a servant of Christ, you can strive to please Him in all you do with the knowledge that no matter what happens, you will never be forsaken. It is easy to give God the glory when you are doing well, but make sure that when things go badly, like losing a close game, you continue to give God the glory. I continued to praise God through my dead senior year and God blessed me by allowing my knee to heal quickly and allowing me to get in the game during our Bowl game.

Live for God in a way that you'll proudly be able to look Him in the eye and say "I have fought the good fight. I have finished the race. I have kept the faith." 2 Timothy 4:7

1. Are you seeking God's favor or the favor of man?

"Am I now trying to win the approval of human beings, or of God? Or am I trying to please people? If I were trying to please people, I would not be a servant of Christ."
Galatians 1:10 (NIV)

"Be strong and courageous. Do not be afraid or terrified
because of them, for the LORD your God goes with you;
he will never leave you nor forsake you."

Deuteronomy 31:6

PREGAME

26

CC BUFORD

GOLF

UNIVERSITY	COLLEGE OF CHARLESTON
HOMETOWN	SAN ANTONIO, TEXAS
JERSEY	N/A
POSITION	N/A
FAVORITE ATHLETE	DAVID ROBINSON AND JORDAN SPIETH
FAVORITE MOVIE	COOL RUNNINGS
FAVORITE ICE CREAM	STRAWBERRY AND COOKIES 'N CREAM
HOBBIES	HIKING, RAFTING, READING, NETFLIX
RANDOM FACT	HIT HOLE IN ONE OFF OPPONENTS BALL

WE IS GREATER THAN ME

Have you ever had a time in your life where you went from being on top of the world and then suddenly found yourself deep in the Marianas Trench? I think we all have this experience, from something as simple as ending middle school and beginning high school. Or it could be something more significant that helps you realize the world does not revolve around you, nor does it fall at your feet. It's a humbling feeling.

This happened to me when I recognized that my high school level of golf was incredibly short of what was expected of me my first semester at college. I went from being a varsity letter athlete at my high school to the youngest player on my college team with, by far, the least developed talent. Nothing discouraged me more than driving to the course every day, knowing I would fail to live up to these expectations.

My fears in practice became rooted in comparing myself to those around me. My motivation was to become better than my teammates even though that goal simply was not realistic. It was not until years later that I read Philippians 2:3-4, and understood that my selfish ambition to be better than my teammates was exactly what was holding me back from having a breakthrough in my golf game and my role as a leader.

Once my reliance on the Lord increased, I was secure in who I was. Not only was I a golfer, I had an identity found in Jesus Christ. The earthly things I had once compared myself to became meaningless next to the joy I found by loving and serving my teammates. His love allowed me to see success in making those around me better, and in these moments, I was able to reflect a servant attitude; the very attitude that Christ embodied in His time here on earth.

1. How can you elevate those around you, whether it's your teammates, siblings, or classmates?

"Do nothing out of selfish ambition or vain conceit. Rather, in humility value others above yourselves, not looking to your own interests but each of you to the interests of others."

Philippians 2:3-4 (NIV)

27

ANNE CAROLINE LOVITT

CHEER

UNIVERSITY	MISSISSIPPI STATE UNIVERSITY
HOMETOWN	HATTIESBURG, MISSISSIPPI
JERSEY	N/A
POSITION	N/A
FAVORITE ATHLETE	NASTIA LIUKEN AND DERRICK ROSE
FAVORITE MOVIE	EMPEROR'S NEW GROOVE
FAVORITE ICE CREAM 	BLUE BELL BANANA PUDDING
HOBBIES 	CLIMBING ANYTHING, DANCING TO MUSIC
RANDOM FACT 	STICKS TONGUE OUT TO CONCENTRATE

THE GIFT OF FAILURE

"Split the V, dot the I, swirl the C, T-O-R-Y! Victory Victory!" That is what cheerleading is all about, right? The "victory." Being a part of MSU's Cheerleading Squad, I saw how fast this talented group developed difficult skills. Things were looking bright for our team.

Despite our bright future, things got cloudy quickly. Practice took us away from our families during Christmas break and struggling to hit stunts during two-a-day practices did not help. The pessimistic plague hit. My coach used to say that the definition of insanity is trying something over and over and expecting different results. He was right, we were all about to go insane.

We showed up at practice everyday, worked hard to hit our routines, but it just never happened. It did not matter how hard we tried, we always seemed to fail. I would tell my teammates to stay positive and believe that we would succeed, but it seemed like success never came. I was confused. I asked God everyday to help us get out of our funk, but our practices were a broken record and we kept struggling.

That is when it hit me. I did not trust the gift giver. Matthew 7:11 says, "If you then who are evil, know how to give good gifts to your children, how much more will your Father who is in heaven give good things to those who ask him!"

God is the ultimate gift-giver. He will not always give you the gift you want, but He will give you the gift you need. I needed the gift of failure to learn perseverance and to learn to lean on my Savior. There was so much pressure from my school, my team and myself. Those pressures led me to put pressure on God to grant me my wish, like He was a genie or something. I learned about the blessings that come when God's answer is "no." God answers prayers to increase faith and to further His kingdom. He cares about what we have to say and wants us to ask him for help.

So the end of this story may not be what you'd expect. You may want to hear that one day it clicked, my team was better than ever, and we won the gold. But in all reality, my team never turned it around, and we did a mediocre job at Nationals. We lost, but what I gained meant so much more. I learned that in Christ, I could be content no matter what the circumstances are. 1 Timothy 6:6 says, " But godliness with contentment is great gain..."

I found peace knowing that in Christ, I'm always on the winning team. An intimacy with Jesus Christ is more precious than any victory, and it outshines any loss.

1. What is that prayer request you think God is not answering? Have you considered the possibility of his answer being "no," or "wait"?

"And my God will meet all your needs according to the riches of his glory in Christ Jesus."
Philippians 4:19 (NIV)

28

EMILY LAMBERT

SOCCER

UNIVERSITY		BRYAN COLLEGE
HOMETOWN		MORRISTOWN, TENNESSEE
JERSEY		#3
POSITION		FORWARD
FAVORITE ATHLETE		ABBY WAMBACH AND ALEX MORGAN
FAVORITE MOVIE		THE LITTLE MERMAID
FAVORITE ICE CREAM		MOOSE TRACKS
HOBBIES		READING AND FROLICKING OUTDOORS
RANDOM FACT		AFRAID OF HEIGHTS

MY GOD, YOUR GOD, OUR GOD

I tore my MCL my senior year of high school and I thought my whole world was crashing down. I fought God hard on why He would allow such a terrible thing to happen to me when I was at the top of my game and planning college visits. My Division 1 aspirations quickly turned into a conundrum: Was competitive soccer even realistic? But God was in total and complete control and during that dark time, I was able to humble myself and see God's purpose when he provided me with the opportunity to play Division II ball.

This wasn't my final destination, The team I was on wasn't spiritually fruitful, and God had His hand on me again when He opened the door for me to transfer to Bryan College. But not even 5 games into the season at my new school, I tore my ACL. Memories from my senior year began to flood all around me and I was quickly reminded of God's love and mercy during that time. Having been through this once before it was much easier to trust in God this time around, and my relationship with Him only grew stronger.

That is the blessing that comes with challenging times; you get the opportunity to place all of your trust in Him. It is easy to get angry at God and ask why bad things are happening to you; but if you can say "show me" instead of asking "why me," you will truly be blessed.

My pastor always said, "God won't bring you to it if He can't get you through it". This reminder is so uplifting, and you begin to realize that if you have the Holy Spirit within you no circumstance is too much. You may be going through a trial, but remain faithful and push through. So keep your head up and praise Him through the storm!

1. How has the Lord blessed you through even the toughest of ordeals?

"Consider it pure joy, my brothers and sisters, whenever you face trials of many kinds."
James 1:2 (NIV)

29

ERIC PETERMAN

FOOTBALL

UNIVERSITY	NORTHWESTERN UNIVERSITY
HOMETOWN	SHERMAN, ILLINOIS
JERSEY	#10
POSITION	RECEIVER
FAVORITE ATHLETE	KURT WARNER AND MICHAEL JORDAN
FAVORITE MOVIE	THE BOURNE TRILOGY
FAVORITE ICE CREAM	PISTACHIO
HOBBIES	TRIATHLONS
RANDOM FACT	NEVER BROKEN A BONE

WHICH PAIN WILL YOU ENDURE?

"You have two choices gentlemen. You can live with the pain of discipline or the pain of regret."

Coach Randy Walker inspired us all with these words during my first preseason camp at Northwestern. This really resonated with me at the time and it still impacts my life today. In conjunction with my life verse, James 1:22, there are three words that I strive to model my life after every single day: Faith, Discipline, Carpe Diem.

College was an immensely busy time for me, as I had to balance athletics and my spiritual life with the normal academic and social aspects of college life that all students experience. Time management was essential along with the will to forge ahead my plan. Through all of this, it was pertinent that I had the discipline to open my Bible every day and make Fellowship of Christian Athletes meetings a priority in my weekly schedule.

Having the pain of discipline to live a Christian life in the midst of my hectic schedule had a significant influence on me, as well as my friends and teammates. God placed me in a unique position to have a platform for showcasing my faith to those around me. If I had not persisted in living a Christian life and striving to be a light for Christ to my teammates, who knows where I would be and what regret I would be experiencing in my life today.

1. What does the pain of discipline look like in your life?

"Do not merely listen to the Word, and so deceive yourselves. Do what it says."
James 1:22 (NIV)

30

CODY PENTECOST

BASEBALL

UNIVERSITY	COLLEGE OF THE OZARKS
HOMETOWN	LEBANON, MISSOURI
JERSEY	#3
POSITION	CENTER-FIELDER
FAVORITE ATHLETE	JIM EDMONDS AND JOSH HAMILTON
FAVORITE MOVIE	42: THE JACKIE ROBINSON STORY
FAVORITE ICE CREAM	STRAWBERRY
HOBBIES	PLAYING GUITAR, PRODUCING MUSIC/VIDEOS
RANDOM FACT	ATTENDS A WORK COLLEGE

CONSTRUCTIVE CRITICISM

I had a coach that was always on everyone's case. It seemed like no one could do anything right. He was a perfectionist. I could have done 9 out of 10 things as perfectly as could be, but the one thing I messed up was always pointed out. I would get so frustrated, thinking "Why doesn't coach just give me a break? I did almost everything right," or, "He doesn't know what he is talking about. I know I'm doing it right."

Growing up, my parents always taught me to respect everyone, especially those that are in authority positions. I learned that God calls us to do the same. Along with respect, there is one other important ingredient that we must have present in our lives: humility. The Bible says in 1 Peter 5:5 to "clothe yourselves with humility." As Christians, we are called to throw aside any pride or selfish ambition. As athletes, we have the ability to accomplish so much, but we must humble ourselves and give God and others the credit for helping us achieve those accomplishments.

After reading that God opposes the proud, I realized that I did not want to be on His opposing side. I do not mind being on the same side of the omnipotent, omniscient, and omnipresent Creator of the universe. I started looking at things a lot differently and seeing them from my coach's perspective. I realized that he was just trying to make me a better ballplayer. If I took his advice, even if it was hard to swallow sometimes, I could see my game improve right before my eyes. Just as we try to strive for perfection in our sport, God calls us to strive for perfection in our relationship with Him. Even though we may fail Him more times than we can count, we must humble ourselves before Him and He will show grace on us.

1. Have you ever had a coach that you thought was a perfectionist? How can your perspective change to honor their authority?

"In the same way, you who are younger, submit yourselves to your elders. All of you, clothe yourselves with humility toward one another, because, 'God opposes the proud but shows favor to the humble'."

1 Peter 5:5 (NIV)

31

GARVIN HAUGHEY

BASKETBALL

UNIVERSITY	INDIANA WESLEYAN UNIVERSITY
HOMETOWN	LEAWOOD, KANSAS
JERSEY	#5
POSITION	SHOOTING GAURD
FAVORITE ATHLETE	KEVIN DURANT AND LUKE RIDNOUR
FAVORITE MOVIE	GLADIATOR
FAVORITE ICE CREAM	COOKIES 'N CREAM
HOBBIES	READING AND MOVIES
RANDOM FACT	DEFINES SUCCESS AS LOOKING GOOD IN GEAR

PLAN FOR PURPOSEFUL EXISTENCE

As an athlete, I despise admitting defeat and displaying weakness. I have experienced quite a bit of both during my collegiate career. I came to Indiana Wesleyan University with the intention of proving that the go–to–guy stud I had been in high school would translate to the next level. I had full confidence that I would shock everyone and dominate from the get–go. But instead I was humbled. A lot. My first day lifting weights with the team I puked my guts out. High school was nothing compared to this.

Physically, I was weak. But I also lacked purpose spiritually. I spent my freshman year on the end of the bench…the far end of the bench. I didn't know how to handle it. I had never warmed the bench before, and I was so caught up in getting credit for being a basketball player that I lost who I truly was in Christ. My identity was wrapped up on the court and my life off the court suffered because of it. It was not until the end my freshmen year that I finally admitted how weak I really was. I was ashamed and I didn't want to talk about the past season.

I finally looked away from basketball and to the Word of God for my worth. This passage was amplified in my life. It didn't matter that I couldn't bench press 225 pounds. It didn't matter that I wasn't seeing the court. I finally found rest in His perfect power. I finally shouted out His name, even though I was weak. I could finally be content, despite the hardship. I finally realized that even though I am weak, I can be made strong because Christ lives in me!

1. What is something in your life that is keeping you from allowing the power of Christ to rest on you?

"But he said to me, 'My grace is sufficient for you, for my power is made perfect in weakness.' Therefore I will boast all the more gladly about my weaknesses, so that Christ's power may rest on me."
2 Corinthians 12:9 (NIV)

GRACE - OLIVIA UNDERWOOD

VOLLEYBALL

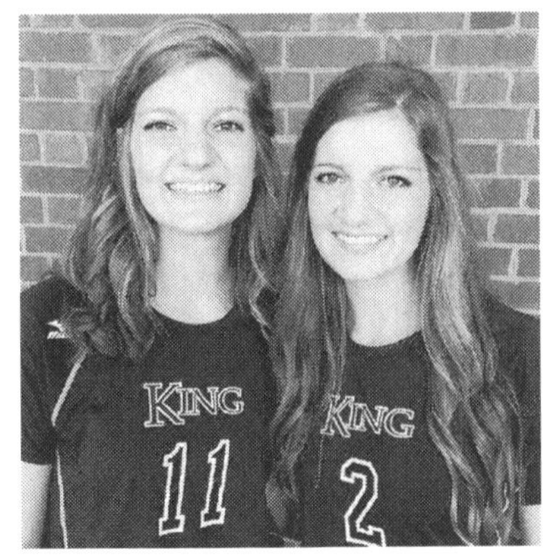

UNIVERSITY	KING UNIVERSITY
HOMETOWN	PEARLAND, TEXAS
JERSEY	#2; #11
POSITION	MIDDLE BLOCKER; SETTER
FAVORITE ATHLETE	HEATHER AND HEIDE BURGE
FAVORITE MOVIE	THE PARENT TRAP AND DESPICABLE ME
FAVORITE ICE CREAM	CHOC. CHIP COOKIE DOUGH; MOOSE TRACKS
HOBBIES	HIKING, CAMPING, CRAFTING, TRAVELING
RANDOM FACT	HAVE SUCCESSFULLY SWITCHED PLACES

THE ETERNAL TROPHY

"The Volleyball Twins" has been our title since the start of our career. We were known as the two look-alikes on the court, which made for tricky game plays and fun team pranks. We are best friends and although we knew the chances were slim, our deepest desire was to spend our college days together. We endured long hours of the recruiting process and fervent prayer until the Lord laid before us a tangible dream. After several people were placed in our lives and many undeniable signs were sent our way, we found ourselves in a small town in Tennessee, 17 hours away from home. One visit was all it took to steal our hearts.

King University became our new home with the leadership of a coach consumed by the spirit and a new family full of sisters in Christ. The King volleyball team has had a legendary motto of, "Our Gifts, His Glory" and we found ourselves playing in the name of the heavenly King.

Our team's main focus is to thrive on these words and honor the Lord by reflecting Christ's love both on and off the court. As we transitioned into a new volleyball season and a new season of our lives, our perspective of the game and athletics in general was suddenly shifted. For a long time, our mindset was on the physical aspect of the game. It is so easy to be exhausted by goals of making it to nationals or to dream of one day appearing on ESPN–the high and mighty trophies of earthly rewards are so attractive to the human eye. However, the honors and pleasures of the world are minuscule in light of eternity.

We have learned that the worth of an eternal perspective is far more valuable than the treasures we collect during our short time here on earth. It is crucial as sons and daughters of God to not find our greatest joys in the temporary, because these things will fade. The Lord intended for sports to be competitive and enjoyable and those are aspects to take delight in; but there is an extent to which our hearts must stay fixed on the prize that lasts forever. Losses are challenging and victories are great, but nothing can compare with the triumph we have in Christ.

1. In what ways have you been consumed with the earthly aspect of athletics?
2. What goals can you set for yourself to have a more eternal perspective?

"But we have this treasure in jars of clay to show that this all-surpassing power is from God and not from us...So we fix our eyes not on what is seen, but on what is unseen, since what is seen is temporary, but what is unseen is eternal."

2 Corinthians 4:7, 18 (NIV)

34

HAYDEN SLACK

FOOTBALL

UNIVERSITY — LOUISIANA TECH FOOTBALL

HOMETOWN — BOSSIER CITY, LOUISIANA

JERSEY — #15

POSITION — WIDE RECEIVER

FAVORITE ATHLETE — TIM TEBOW

FAVORITE MOVIE — ROCKY IV

FAVORITE ICE CREAM — REESE'S PEANUT BUTTER CUP

HOBBIES — ANYTHING RELATED TO SPORTS

RANDOM FACT — LOVES RUNNING

WAS THE GOOD BOOK WRITTEN ABOUT YOU?

Behind any great team, there is great leadership. I've seen it several times where one person has either had a positive or negative affect on the whole dynamic of a team.

My junior year we went into the season with high expectations, believing we had the potential to win a conference championship. But we started off the season 1-4 and selfishness began to creep in. Everyone had already packed it in that our championship season was not attainable; but a few teammates completely transformed the mental makeup of our squad.

I will never forget how they stood up and promised to dedicate themselves to the team instead of themselves as individuals. Our team understood the message: its not about me, it's about us! We went on to win seven straight games and captured that conference championship.

Our motivation reveals the character of our ambitions. In the Bible, we see the true example of leadership from the life of one man, Jesus Christ. He did not just tell us how to lead, he emptied himself and showed us how to lead. Jesus became a servant and ultimately died on the cross in our place for the punishment of our sins. He was the type of leader that all of his disciples were willing to die for.

Humility is not a sign of weakness, but rather a sign of great strength that can only be found in Christ. Humility is not thinking less of yourself. It is thinking of yourself less. Jesus commands that if anyone is to follow him they must deny themselves. In order for Jesus to increase in our lives, we must decrease.

We cannot know how to lead until we personally know Jesus Christ as our Lord and Savior. Submit your life to him today and he will show you how to lead so that others will follow.

1. Is your motivation for being a leader self–centered or Christ-centered?

"He must become greater; I must become less."
John 3:30 (NIV)

35

LANDON WACHTER

CROSS-COUNTRY - TRACK

UNIVERSITY — UNIVERSITY OF MISSOURI

HOMETOWN — JACKSON, MISSOURI

JERSEY — N/A

POSITION — EVENT: 800 METER

FAVORITE ATHLETE — MARIA EFFINGER

FAVORITE MOVIE — THE SOUND OF MUSIC

FAVORITE ICE CREAM — CHOCOLATE FROM ANDY'S

HOBBIES — JESUS, COFFEE, NETFLIX

RANDOM FACT  LOVES ESSENTIAL OILS

CONTENTMENT

The simple but powerful verse Philippians 4:13, "I can do all things through Him who strengthens me," seems to be a theme for all athletes whether they live for Jesus or not. However, the two verses before this famous verse have taught me what it means to say that I can do all things through Him who strengthens me.

In verse 11, Paul says he has learned to be "content in whatever circumstance" he was in, whether that was prosperity, humility, hunger or abundance. The word contentment is defined as being satisfied with what one is or has, not wanting more or anything else.

As athletes, we have all experienced these different circumstances Paul is talking about. Sometimes we are having a great season and are living in prosperity. We are successful in our sport, school is going awesome and everything in life seems to be going our way. In contrast, we have all endured the seasons where God humbles us and we seem to encounter every trial possible. Trials such as injury, sickness, school being overwhelming, or things in life are not that great.

Just like us, Paul has encountered different seasons in his life, but he says he has learned to be content in having everything and in having nothing. If we find our contentment in things of this world such as our sport, success, school, people, etc, we will always be searching for something to fill us and will never truly be content. Paul tells us that to truly be content, we must not worry about what or how much we have, but about who has our hearts. If we rest in God for contentment, whenever we encounter seasons of prosperity and those tough seasons of trials, only then can we truly say that, "I can do all things through Him who strengthens me."

1. What changes can you make in your life to make sure you are content in any and every circumstance?

"I am not saying this because I am in need, for I have learned to be content whatever the circumstances. I know what it is to be in need, and I know what it is to have plenty. I have learned the secret of being content in any and every situation, whether well fed or hungry, whether living in plenty or in want. I can do all this through him who gives me strength."

Philippians 4:11-13 (NIV)

36

GRANT SHEWEY

TENNIS

UNIVERSITY  TABOR COLLEGE

HOMETOWN  HILLSBORO, KANSAS

JERSEY N/A

POSITION  N/A

FAVORITE ATHLETE  ADRIAN PETERSON

FAVORITE MOVIE  LION KING

FAVORITE ICE CREAM  CHOCOLATE CHIP COOKIE DOUGH

HOBBIES 
BIKING, PING PONG, ULTIMATE FRISBEE

RANDOM FACT  ONE DAY OLDER THAN JUSTIN BIEBER

WE BEFORE ME

My high school always asserted that working hard and winning for them would lead to gratification and satisfaction. As time went on, I found this type of attitude to be extremely superficial and it significantly contributed to me competing as a college athlete for only a semester. I grew weary of consuming myself in my performance and I lacked genuine concern for my teammates. So I decided to step aside in order to get my attitude and priorities straight.

I have always felt like I have a gift for being an energetic and positive person, but you would not know it if you saw me in competition. I allowed my pride and selfish ambition to keep me from impacting others with an infectious mindset that resembles Christ. Since then, when I have made an effort to direct my enthusiasm toward others first, it has made all of the difference. Athletics are a great way to use constructive enthusiasm to spur others into playing for more than themselves.

Ultimately, if we are going to live with eternal perspectives, then the results of athletic competition are minimal compared to what God can do through such a platform. The simple fact that we are all alive and able to compete on a daily basis is easy to take for granted. Do not let a selfish outlook keep you from loving on your teammates, and inspiring them so that they may see the joy of Christ in you.

1. Who around you can you encourage and lift up today?

"Serve wholeheartedly, as if you were serving the LORD, not people."
Ephesians 6:7 (NIV)

37

LAUREN CARTMELL

GYMNASTICS

UNIVERSITY	LINDENWOOD UNIVERSITY
HOMETOWN	AURORA, COLORADO
JERSEY	N/A
POSITION	ALL-AROUND
FAVORITE ATHLETE	NASTIA LIUKEN AND PAUL HAMM
FAVORITE MOVIE	REMEMBER THE TITANS
FAVORITE ICE CREAM	COOKIES 'N CREAM
HOBBIES	SCARPBOOKING, MODELING, DANCING
RANDOM FACT	LOVES WORKING OUT TO JUSTIN BIEBER

LOSING IS WINNING

The summer prior to my sophomore year, I attended an amazing Christian athlete camp and entered the school year beyond ecstatic to start training with a different purpose, —to glorify God unlike I ever had before.

But after only a few months into preseason, I had hit rock bottom. My nerves were adversely impacting my performance, so much so that my coach pulled me aside and told me that if I did not pull myself together, he would have to reconsider my position on the team.

It was all slipping out of my grasp, as if there was nothing I could do about it. I was losing, and losing it. But it was this very loss that helped me gain Him again.

I realized that I was once again putting my identity in my sport. I had gone into each practice praying that God would help me succeed and asking for specific things that I wanted instead of praying for His glory, His will. That same day, I went home and spoke with one of my old coaches. "Don't you remember all that you learned at camp this summer?" she said. "You must put all your trust in God, and He will guide you".

As I took some time to reflect, I began to dwell on Joshua 1:9. Why am I afraid? God is by my side at all times and with Him I am free from all anxieties. I do not need to put my focus on my thoughts, I just need to lift them up to God.

1. What are some fears or obstacles that you have tried to overcome without the help of God?

"Have I not commanded you? Be strong and courage. Do not be afraid; do not be discouraged, for the Lord your God will be with you wherever you go."
Joshua 1:9 (NIV)

38

JAKE VAN GILSE

FOOTBALL

UNIVERSITY	TAYLOR UNIVERSITY
HOMETOWN	BATAVIA, ILLINOIS
JERSEY	#17
POSITION	KICKER/PUNTER
FAVORITE ATHLETE	ROBBIE GOULD
FAVORITE MOVIE	GLADIATOR
FAVORITE ICE CREAM	ANY CHOCOLATE AND PEANUT BUTTER COMBO
HOBBIES	READING, BOARD GAMES, PING PONG
RANDOM FACT	GLUTEN-FREE SINCE 2010

GIVE IT ALL - HE DID

The pitfalls of mediocrity as a student–athlete are abundant. We not only seek to maintain a commitment of excellence to our studies in the classroom, since most of us know that our time on the field will soon be over, but also to our athletic endeavors. But we also strive to influence our teammates as well.

As the initial excitement and joy that follows the start of a new year quickly gives way to the stress and exhaustion of the mid–semester grind, the easy way out seems to beckon relentlessly. It creeps up on us in the simplest of ways, ending up five minutes late to class just so you could hit that snooze button one more time, or convincing yourself you've completed all ten repetitions in your lifting set when you know full well that you've only done nine. In these seemingly innocent moments, our character is tested, strained and falters eventually, as this lapse of integrity consumes our lives. Soon we are skipping class, confident that our status as a "superstar athlete" will excuse us. Grades then begin to dwindle, and our stay in the weight room is shortened by a few minutes with each successive visit.

Integrity can be described as faithfulness inspired by love. Faithfulness by itself builds a rigid form of strict obedience and adherence to a set of rules and regulations. But, when faithfulness is inspired by love, it is strengthened to become a joyful compliance, intending to please the Lord who gave us everything.

I, like many others, struggled through countless injuries during my collegiate career. During these times I had two choices; continue to go to morning workouts and encourage the team, or sleep in, going unnoticed all the while. (Kickers have an innate ability to be slightly invisible.)

My choice to remain faithful to my commitment to my teammates gave me opportunities to foster relationships and increase my love for my brothers–in–Christ. Righteousness in the midst of struggle builds a pattern of character that will serve as a foundation of excellence for every area of your life. Stand firm, conquer the daily battles of mediocrity, and build a reputation of honor!

1. How can you seek reconciliation in your mistakes and reclaim integrity?

"And the LORD said to Satan, 'Have you considered my servant Job? There is no one on earth like him; he is blameless and upright, a man who fears God and shuns evil. And he still maintains his integrity, though you incited me against him to ruin him without any reason.'"

Job 2:3 (NIV)

39

GABBY DYER

SOCCER

UNIVERSITY	MARSHALL UNIVERSITY
HOMETOWN	FALLS CHURCH, VIRGINIA
JERSEY	#30
POSITION	OUTSIDE MIDFIELDER
FAVORITE ATHLETE	GABBY DOUGLAS AND LIONEL MESSI
FAVORITE MOVIE	LAW ABIDING CITIZEN
FAVORITE ICE CREAM	COFFEE FLAVORED
HOBBIES	WORKING OUT AND DANCING
RANDOM FACT	CAN'T STAND FEET

MORE VALUABLE THAN FAME

As athletes, I am sure we have all encountered that one individual who appears to have it made. They are a superstar on the field, can do nothing wrong in the coaches' eyes, win accolades galore and yet do not walk with Christ in the slightest. If someone does not come to mind, consider the world's most prominent sports figures. So many of them flaunt promiscuity and openly reject God, yet continue to grow in fame and own the most expensive cars, boats, and jets. They are seen laughing and dancing at the club and surrounded by multitudes of friends. They are the "in–crowd."

I can attest to the fact that this is extremely frustrating to deal with as a Christian athlete. Especially as a new Christian, it is troubling to go from the excitement of finding everlasting love and grace in Christ, to realizing that your life does not suddenly transform into a fairytale.

Oftentimes, life after becoming a Christian gets harder. People who you considered closest to you will abandon you. Others judge you and the life you used to lead may seem tempting. In this situation, it is extremely difficult to see the big picture and trust that God has tremendous plans of prosperity and happiness for you. You may ask yourself, "What's the point in trying to live a holy life and restricting myself when it means I can't have any fun?"

If you find yourself asking this question and find that your "steps had nearly slipped," read Psalm 73. Those who are unfaithful to the Lord, like the arrogant athlete with all the world's most valuable possessions, will perish. But you, a child of God, have the most valuable gift that anyone could ever receive: an eternal relationship with Jesus. Through Him you will find everlasting life in heaven, with a multitude of others; life far beyond the parties, clubs, and bars here on earth. Though our flesh may fail us, God is our ever–present source of strength and continually who shapes our desires according to His.

1. What does this world have to offer that is more valuable than eternal life with Christ?

"But as for me, my feet had almost slipped; I had nearly lost my foothold...Those who are far from you will perish; you destroy all who are unfaithful to you. But as for me, it is good to be near God. I have made the Sovereign Lord my refuge; I will tell of all your deeds."

Psalm 73:2, 27-28 (NIV)

40

DAVID FUENTES

BASEBALL

UNIVERSITY  TABOR COLLEGE

HOMETOWN CORONA, CALIFORNIA

JERSEY  #43

POSITION  FIRST BASE; THIRD BASE; OUTFIELDER

FAVORITE ATHLETE  ALBERT PUJOLS AND BRANCH WARREN

FAVORITE MOVIE  LORD OF THE RINGS: TWO TOWERS

FAVORITE ICE CREAM  COOKIES 'N CREAM

HOBBIES WEIGHTLIFTING, PIANO, BEATBOXING

RANDOM FACT  AWESOME GUITARIST IN GAME ROCK BAND

WE ALL NEED MORE THAN WHEATIES

I remember waking up every single day anxious about what that day would hold. Baseball was in season and I was overbooked: a heavy school schedule of upper level classes, Resident Assistant duties, practice, games, small groups, and striving to maintain something of a social life. Talk about hectic! Constantly surrounded by people and trying to please my peers and coach every waking moment of the day was wearing me down. Being 1,500 miles away from home, I also worried about my family. I would sometimes ask God why it all had to be so difficult. I was instantly overwhelmed each day as I thought of all that had to be done. It all finally came to a head and I cried out, "God! If you can hear me, I just need to know you are with me!"

Well, let's just say that He definitely heard me, like always. In a small group that next week we were challenged to dive into God's word as soon as we got up, reading a few verses daily and spending a while in prayer. I hit this challenge head on, and I can't believe what a difference it made in my life. I felt like I was talking to God as if He were right next to me, and I could tell Him anything. All of my worries seemed to disappear when I would start the day out right. It provided me with the right mindset each day, giving me time to clear any negative thoughts. There is just something so fulfilling when you learn to take your thoughts to Him, with no one around; just you and Him and peace.

1. What are some thoughts that cause you stress?

"Very early in the morning, while it was still dark, Jesus got up, left the house and went off to a solitary place, where he prayed."

Mark 1:35 (NIV)

41

CONNOR BAXTER

WRESTLING

UNIVERSITY OKLAHOMA STATE UNIVERSITY

HOMETOWN TULSA, OKLAHOMA

JERSEY N/A

POSITION WEIGHT CLASS: 149

FAVORITE ATHLETE ADAM DONYES

FAVORITE MOVIE THE SANDLOT

FAVORITE ICE CREAM CHOCOLATE CHIP COOKIE DOUGH

HOBBIES SKATE, WAKE, AND SNOW BOARDING

RANDOM FACT DREAM JOB INVOLVES FIREFIGHTING

SPORT = WORSHIP

Too often I have fallen into the mindset that I have to be at church to worship God. Or even more so, I have to be singing certain songs that we refer to as "worship". This mindset can get me in a lot of trouble.

When we limit worship to Sunday morning we also limit our interaction and intimacy with God, and ultimately diminish the Gospel. Why? We do this despite Jesus dying for our sins. He paid for them completely and imputed to us his righteousness. No longer do we have to go to a temple and sacrifice animals to be in the right standing with God and have a fruitful relationship with Him as they did in the Old Testament. This now allows us all to have full communication and intimacy with God, thereby allowing us to worship him wherever. This applies if you are on a wrestling mat, basketball court, football field, or wherever else life takes you; you are just as much with God and worshiping Him as you are on a Sunday morning. Don't forget Hebrews 13:5 that tells us He will never leave us, nor will He ever forsake us.

Society (especially the sporting world) often conditions us to be of the "go–getter" mentality. If you want something, you've got to make it happen. The thought process is simple; I have to do this and this and this to get this. "If I want to win a National Title, I have to practice every day, out–work everyone else, eat right, not indulge in anything that will hinder my performance…" The list goes on and on.

This is a thought process every athlete has to have, but I warn you not to let this carry over into your spiritual life, for this goes against the Gospel. We were saved by grace through faith and we can never earn salvation. We must work to provide for our families, reach our goals, and better the world. But not salvation. It is a gift from God, for all of us. One that we should treasure.

1. When we limit worship to Sunday morning we also limit our interaction and intimacy with God, and ultimately diminish the Gospel. Why do we do this?

"Therefore, I urge you, brothers and sisters, in the view of God's mercy, to offer your bodies as a living sacrifice, holy and pleasing to God — this is your true and proper worship."

Romans 12:1 (NIV)

42

JARED BEEKMAN

FOOTBALL

UNIVERSITY	JOHNS HOPKINS UNIVERSITY
HOMETOWN	SAINT CLOUD, FLORIDA
JERSEY	#18
POSITION	WIDE RECEIVER
FAVORITE ATHLETE	PEYTON MANNING AND DREW BREES
FAVORITE MOVIE	EVERY JAMES BOND MOVIE
FAVORITE ICE CREAM	STRAWBERRY CHEESECAKE
HOBBIES	WAKEBOARDING, GUITAR, CORNHOLE
RANDOM FACT	HAS EXTRA CREASE ON BOTH RING FINGERS

AN IDENTITY OF INTEGRITY

Entering college my freshman year I looked for an identity and was curious about all the changes that living on my own would have in store. Being the first group of students on campus in the fall, my teammates became my first friends; so naturally the idea of being in a fraternity (termed WaWa - don't ask!) that provided a sense of belonging intrigued me. Yet, I also knew that the lifestyle that was ingrained in WaWa severely clashed with my Christian values. This would be the beginning of a major internal conflict in my life. I told myself that if God was really the center of my life, no matter where I ended up, He would be there to guide me and direct me to the path of righteousness. But was this really the case, or was I just using that as an excuse to live my own life?

So there I was, worried that joining WaWa would threaten my integrity as a Christian, while at the same time, trying to shape my identity as "one of the guys". In Luke, Chapter 16, Jesus paints the perfect picture of both integrity and identity. In the parable of the unjust steward, Jesus explains that we cannot serve two masters and that our actions in this world have direct consequences on our relationship with God.

Christ is the epitome of integrity. He left His comfort zone to preach to sinners, a "transgression" that resulted in Him being mocked and beaten, and hung on the cross. Yet never once did He turn away from God. Through His example, I knew that I needed to form my identity in Christ and needed to reach out to my teammates as well. God was calling me to be a positive influence on them, rather than them being a negative influence on me.

In the end, I decided not to join the fraternity. I have, however, learned not to shun WaWa or condemn a certain lifestyle, but rather invite my teammates to live in the light of Christ. It hasn't been easy, but God's grace has given me strength to leave my own comfort zone and strive to live for Him.

1. Does my lifestyle reflect Christ in every environment, not just at church or small group?

"Whoever can be trusted with very little can also be trusted with much, and whoever is dishonest with very little will also be dishonest with much."

Luke 16:10 (NIV)

43

JAKE BARNETT

BASKETBALL

UNIVERSITY	SAINT LOUIS UNIVERSITY
HOMETOWN	WAUWATOSA, WISCONSIN
JERSEY	#30
POSITION	GUARD
FAVORITE ATHLETE	TIM TEBOW
FAVORITE MOVIE	ANCHORMAN
FAVORITE ICE CREAM	CHERRY
HOBBIES	SPORTS
RANDOM FACT	HUGE ST. LOUIS FAN

SPIRITUAL BATTLE IN COMPETITION

I have read Ephesians 6:12 numerous times and meditated on what it really means. I ask myself if there is really a spiritual battle taking place all around me? Are there angels battling demons in my defense as I walk to class or as I prepare for a game? To many, this may seem a little overwhelming. What does Paul actually mean when he says our battle is not against flesh and blood?

Recently, my prayer as I walk onto the court has become, "Lord, let me win the spiritual battle tonight." What does winning the spiritual battle mean to me? It means that when something does not go my way I show positive determination, an example of Christ's love, over cursing and getting angry. It means that when my coach yells at me, I choose to respectfully listen rather than dismiss his authority in my life. It means that in the heat of battle, I am fully submitting to Christ and allowing His ever-present grace and light to shine through me.

After a recent game, (which we won) I found myself once again, like many athletes, being my own biggest critic. On the way home, I vented to my fiancée about numerous things I thought I could have done better. As usual, she listened with grace and tried to sympathize with my disappointment. However, right before we walked into my house, I stopped and looked her in the face and said, "On a bright note, I didn't curse like I usually do. Definitely felt like I won that spiritual battle tonight." My fiancée affirmed me and we rejoiced in my personal victory.

More than anything, Christ wants to further His kingdom through us. He desires us to share the love and grace He shows us with others. Remember that the battle we face is not of this world. I am the most competitive person you will ever meet, but I constantly have to ask myself: Is winning a basketball game more important than being an ambassador of Christ? And the answer is always no.

One tactic I use to remind myself to be aware of the more important battle, is to imagine Jesus himself sitting in an empty arena chair watching me play. He is my biggest fan! No matter what happens in the heat of the game, Christ looks upon me with grace and love. He knows my identity isn't found in the win or loss column, but rather as His chosen, adopted son of Christ.

1. Do you recognize the spiritual battle that takes place during competition?

"For our struggle is not against flesh and blood, but against the rulers, against the authorities, against the powers of this dark world and against the spiritual forces of evil in the heavenly realms."
Ephesians 6:12 (NIV)

44

MARY BETH HOWARD

SWIMMING AND DIVING

UNIVERSITY	U. OF ILLINOIS - URBANA-CHAMPAIGN
HOMETOWN	ST. LOUIS, MISSOURI
JERSEY	N/A
POSITION	N/A
FAVORITE ATHLETE	MICHAEL PHELPS AND MISSY FRANKLIN
FAVORITE MOVIE	IRON MAN
FAVORITE ICE CREAM	CARAMEL
HOBBIES	BAKING AND CRAFTING
RANDOM FACT	LOVES POPCORN

GIFTS FROM A GIVING GOD

Athletes (and people in general, really) are constantly under pressure. Coming into college, I had no idea what responsibilities were ahead of me. I was a captain of the Swim and Dive team in high school and made good grades, but this was an entirely new experience for me.

Freshman year was a rough one. From the outset, not only was I the weakest person on the team, but I was also struggling academically. In addition, my longtime boyfriend and I had just ended our relationship. Needless to say, I felt as if the weight of all of this was crushing me.

During that time, and for a while after that, if you were to ask me to describe myself, I would say "weary and burdened". I continued to feel the stress of these trials until I truly gave these burdens to God. Before I surrendered to him, I was thinking about quitting the sport that I love and switching majors, anything in order to turn my life around.

But the Bible says to us, "present your requests to God", surrender your worries and troubles, and God will give you rest. He shielded me from my stress just as a parent does for their child.

Since then, life as a student-athlete has become one of the most fun and rewarding experiences that I could ever imagine. When I have a big meet or an exam coming up, I ask God for His strength and courage, and His peace and comfort wash over me like a breath of relief. He will never fail you.

1. How has God helped you deal with the pressures in your life?

"Come to me, all you who are weary and burdened, and I will give you rest."
Mathew 11:28 (NIV)

45

KAYLA WALTON

VOLLEYBALL

UNIVERSITY 	MISSOURI STATE UNIVERSITY
HOMETOWN 	TAMPA, FLORIDA
JERSEY 	#1
POSITION 	RIGHT SIDE HITTER
FAVORITE ATHLETE 	PEYTON MANNING AND KERRI WALSH
FAVORITE MOVIE 	THE BLIND SIDE
FAVORITE ICE CREAM 	COOKIE DOUGH
HOBBIES 	WORKING OUT, MUSIC, COFFEE SHOPS
RANDOM FACT 	GRADUATED IN 3 YEARS

NEVER BACK DOWN

Sustaining a severe knee injury in high school amidst aspirations of playing college ball is tough. The day I tore my ACL is one that I will not forget. I proceeded to have three surgeries in two months, but it was worth it. I registered a full recovery after eight long months. It felt as if I would never heal, but I placed my full trust in God. He never led me astray.

The recruiting process was hard on me, especially when colleges backed off due to my injury, but one school, the University of South Florida, maintained interest.

When preseason rolled around my family suffered an unexpected loss and I went down again—the same leg. It seemed like my dreams of playing college athletics were being squashed after just two practices.

"What is my identity now?" was all I kept asking myself. Despite all the numerous medical professionals advising me not to play, I placed all of my pain and fear in God and kept on the path.

With a full season under my belt, it became clear that God was not done testing me. He put a forth obstacle in front of me that required that I put all of my strength in Him if I was to succeed. I was told that I would never be allowed to run again. My coaches were willing to work with me and were more than understanding when I could not practice. All of the sweat and toil eventually led me to earning all-conference accolades in the Big East my junior year.

God will never put you through more than you can handle. Christ always has a plan for you and wants you to succeed while honoring Him on and off the court. I write Philippians 4:13 on my wrist before every game and play for the one who has given me the talent and fortitude to succeed day in and day out.

1. Is my relationship with God strong enough to the point that I will curb all of my fear and follow him?

"I can do all this through him who gives me strength."
Philippians 4:13 (NIV)

46

JUSTIN BRITT

FOOTBALL

UNIVERSITY	UNIVERSITY OF MISSOURI
HOMETOWN	FORT CAMPBELL, KENTUCKY
JERSEY	#68
POSITION	LINEMAN
FAVORITE ATHLETE	KOBY BRYANT
FAVORITE MOVIE	TED
FAVORITE ICE CREAM	ROCKY ROAD
HOBBIES	SPENDING TIME WITH FAMILY
RANDOM FACT	LARGEST BABY BORN IN KENTUCKY- 11 LBS

WHAT'S YOUR PRIZE?

Life is about "running." I do not say that just because personally, playing football for a living, my daily routine happens to involve a lot of running. It is not that kind of running I'm talking about. What I'm referring to has nothing to do with rapidly putting one foot in front of the other, physically willing yourself to your destination. Rather, I'm talking about running being a spiritual race which we are all running.

Every day of our lives, we are "running" somewhere. Each person is born with an innate need to accomplish something. What someone strives to achieve differs greatly based on an individual's view of success and the meaning of one's life. Some aspire to reap great riches, public admiration, or a combination of the two. But, as 1 Corinthians 9:24 clearly states, there is only one prize at the finish line. Everyone is pining for that prize; Jesus and His heavenly kingdom. To obtain this prize, we must run our spiritual races for Him and put all our energy into doing His will and following His commands.

1 Corinthians 9:24 tells us that if you run the race for Him, there is no telling what is possible. At this time last year, I was studying for the last round of final exams of my college career. Nine months later, I was studying the New England Patriots' defense in preparation for Super Bowl XLIX.

Now let me ask you, how did I, a normal guy from a small Missouri town, become not only the starting lineman for the Missouri Tigers and the Seattle Seahawks, but also climb atop the football world in my rookie year? By running after God. It is something I will be able to tell my beautiful baby girl someday and share with her what can happen when you trust in the Lord and pursue God. He will deliver. Always.

1. In the race for God, you can only do two things: Run closer to Him, or drift further away. Which one are you doing?

"Do you not know that in a race all the runners run, but only one gets the prize? Run in such a way as to get the prize."
1 Corinthians 9:24 (NIV)

47

LEAH CONNERY

SOCCER

UNIVERSITY	WILLIAM JEWELL COLLEGE
HOMETOWN	KEARNEY, MISSOURI
JERSEY	#17
POSITION	MIDFIELDER
FAVORITE ATHLETE	BRANDI CHASTAIN
FAVORITE MOVIE	42
FAVORITE ICE CREAM	VANILLA
HOBBIES	TIME WITH FAMILY, AND BAKING
RANDOM FACT	IN HIGH SCHOOL BASKETBALL SHOT AT WRONG BASKET AND MADE IT THREE TIMES.

PATIENCE ON THE PITCH

Looking at the whiteboard, my eyes burned with anguish. My mind raced to everything I must have done wrong. I considered things that I needed to improve. I just had to recapture my starting spot. Every game of the season began the same way; I would see the numbers on the whiteboard, my jersey number nowhere to be seen.

Regretfully, this utter disappointment claimed my happiness in these moments. I let the game become my stress reliever, my sense of joy, my go to. But my one-time source of contentment had now become my source of affliction. It was then that my patience began to be tested.

I yearned to know more. Where did patience on the field begin? Was it something accomplished once or was it a daily struggle? I could not pinpoint the answer until I remembered why I was still playing this game.

It began with my first pass of the ball, the first practice at five years old when I did not have a lick of experience. Before I knew it, patience intertwined itself into every moment on the field. I chose it during the game, not only for the little girl who dreamed of playing collegiate ball, but also for the undying love of the game. I found my love somewhere between learning how to wear my shin guards and the sensation of orange slices at halftime.

Now, after years of personal success, patience found me in a different manner—from the bench. I had to believe in the idea that my needs, my wants and my timing took a back seat to His. What kept me going was keeping Psalm 46:10; close to my heart and in the forefront of my mind.

I find peace in knowing that my stillness would honor the One that I need approval from, the Lord. Even in the whirlwind of dwindling patience, it is the tranquility He offers through faith and the calling to be a woman of God that rests above all else.

1. What are three verses you can turn to when your patience is slipping away?

"He says, 'Be still, and know that I am God; I will be exalted among the nations, I will be exalted in the earth.'"

Psalm 46:10 (NIV)

48

ERIN GILLILAND

BASEBALL

UNIVERSITY	ABILENE CHRISTIAN UNIVERSITY
HOMETOWN	MIDLAND, TEXAS
JERSEY	#8
POSITION	CATCHER
FAVORITE ATHLETE	DUSTIN PEDROIA AND JURICKSON PROFAR
FAVORITE MOVIE	42
FAVORITE ICE CREAM	PEANUT BUTTER CUP PERFECTION
HOBBIES	ANYTHING OUTDOORS
RANDOM FACT	VEGAN FOR 6 MONTHS AND COUNTING

HALF TRUTHS

My whole life had been planned out. When I would get married, where I would live, my future job, how many kids I would have, everything down to the most intricate detail had been meticulously sorted through and discussed. I was completely confident in the plans that were so carefully created and the one with whom I created them. As I was about to embark on a brand new journey, transferring from a junior college to Abilene Christian University to play softball, every detail that was so carefully planned disintegrated in the blink of an eye. I was bitter. I was broken. I swore to myself that I would never be in such a vulnerable position EVER again.

To say that I guarded my heart would be the understatement of the century. Alarms would sound, lights would flash, and I would retreat in the opposite direction with a full-on sprint if anyone even became remotely close. In the midst of this full-on rebellion, the Lord was the last thing on my mind. He planted Proverbs 4:23 in my head: "Above all else guard your heart, for everything you do flows from it." But I used it completely out of context, icing my heart over to "protect" it, which is exactly what the world screams.

Satan loves half-truths. He feeds off them. The world is full of broken promises, lies, and hurt. On our own, we become bitter just as I was. The full truth, though, is that God does not want our hearts to be iced over. It is His job to protect them and not ours.

It was through that experience that God revealed so much truth about who He is. He is our protector. He is our warrior. He is our comforter. He is our healer. Most importantly though, He is our savior. Sometimes it takes failure on our own to realize that He saves us from the world, the devil and even our sinful nature.

1. What is holding you back from completely trusting God with your heart?

"Above all else, guard your heart, for everything you do flows from it"
Proverbs 4:23 (NIV)

49

MANDY PERKINS

TRACK

UNIVERSITY	UNIVERSITY OF FLORIDA
HOMETOWN	DAYTONA BEACH, FLORIDA
JERSEY	N/A
POSITION	EVENT: MILE; 800 METERS
FAVORITE ATHLETE	LOPEZ LOMONG AND CHRIS KLUWE
FAVORITE MOVIE	THE PERKS OF BEING A WALLFLOWER
FAVORITE ICE CREAM	CHOCOLATE PEANUT BUTTER
HOBBIES	PLAYING THE PIANO
RANDOM FACT	WAS ADOPTED INTO AN AMAZING FAMILY

DIRECTING THE GLORY

Some have questioned why I have credited God with pushing me to work so hard in order to win races. My thanks to Him has also been met with resistance and anger.

"That's ridiculous," they often say. "God didn't run those miles for you. He didn't run all of those hours and feel the resulting pain. That was all you; 'praying' doesn't equal effort."

I cannot believe folks would say something like this. God moves so much in our lives each and every single day!

God is our personal Heavenly coach. He never leaves our side, even after practice. He is the adrenaline in our veins and the oxygen in our lungs. He is there every step of the way, the little voice in our head screaming "Don't give up!" How could we NOT credit Him?

God blessed us with our talent and our athleticism. He gave us these abilities for a purpose, to cause others to look to us for guidance. The least we can do in exchange for our abilities and accolades is to stay humble and please Him. So the next time someone praises you for your talent, do exactly this, and shed some light on God!

1. What are some ways that you can thank God for your success and failures?

"Be completely humble and gentle; be patient, bearing with one another in love."
Ephesians 4:2 (NIV)

50

KEVIN DOMINGUE

FOOTBALL

UNIVERSITY		HOWARD PAYNE UNIVERSITY
HOMETOWN		LAKE DALLAS, TEXAS
JERSEY		#12
POSITION		RECEIVER
FAVORITE ATHLETE		COLT MCCOY AND TIM TEBOW
FAVORITE MOVIE		FRIDAY NIGHT LIGHTS
FAVORITE ICE CREAM		PIZOOKIE
HOBBIES		CAMPING, BIKING, PING PONG
RANDOM FACT		MATH IS HIS FAVORITE SUBJECT

TRAINING FOR ETERNITY

How much effort do we give to be great at our sport? As a child that grew up playing sports and now as a college football player, I have devoted countless hours to competition and preparation for it. Athletes train for years to prepare for the one moment when they are able to be at their absolute best and, hopefully, achieve victory. We push our bodies in the weight room and on the track to become as fast and as strong as we are capable of during the off-season, with our eyes set on an approaching game day.

Although giving our all in preparation and competition is important, and asked of us by Christ in Colossians 3:23 for His glory, however, we have to remember that it is still only for a worldly prize, a trophy that can break or for bragging rights that will be worthless at the end of time.

Christ has set us free from this world and calls us to live for more than the trivial things. In 1 Timothy 4:8, we are told that godliness exceeds all other talents, abilities, or skills because it is the only thing that will remain for eternity, into the eternal life to come in the presence of God. We should train our minds in Christ in a way that shows He is the ultimate victory in our lives.

I often step back and examine my life to see if I am truly giving the same effort in training for godliness as I am in training for football. Sadly, I realize that I have my priorities out of line. Luckily for me and you alike, Jesus loves us through these failures and relentlessly pursues our hearts daily. Today, realize that if you're a Christian you carry the name of Jesus and should give 100 percent in all you do to glorify Him. But also know that Christ wants your all in a personal relationship with Him.

1. Would your life look any different if you gave more effort in becoming Godly than you do in training for your sport?

"For physical training is of some value, but godliness has value for all things, holding promise for both the present life and the life to come."
1 Timothy 4:8 (NIV)

51

JOE DEATHRAGE

TENNIS

UNIVERSITY	OKLAHOMA WESLEYAN UNIVERSITY
HOMETOWN	MOORE, OKLAHOMA
JERSEY	N/A
POSITION	#2 DOUBLES; #4 SINGLES
FAVORITE ATHLETE	JOHN ISNER AND THE BRYAN BROTHERS
FAVORITE MOVIE	TO SAVE A LIFE
FAVORITE ICE CREAM	MINT CHOCOLATE CHIP
HOBBIES	RUNNING, WATCHING HIGHSCHOOL SPORTS
RANDOM FACT	NEVER SEEN ANY OF THE BATMAN MOVIES

WHAT GOD DESIRES

First things first: I absolutely love tennis. For a good portion of my life, it was all I could think about. But it was not until I had progressed to the collegiate level and was mentored by a magnificent MOG (man of God) and coach that I realized that every tournament or award I had won ultimately meant nothing. I had been playing for myself, and myself only.

My junior year I made a pact with God that my uniform is His uniform from there on out. Every time I step on the court I would play for Him and show what a Christian athlete looks like.

You would think that more blessings in the form of trophies, accolades and awards would start to drop from the heavens after such a proclamation. Well, that season turned out to be my worst to date. I will admit that it stirred doubt: "I'm following God now, so why did I struggle so much?"

The summer after that season was so impactful. I was surrounded by God's beauty and some great guys as well. Additionally, I had a lot of time by myself to reflect on the past year. I realized that my heart's desires should not be of worldly things. Rather, they should consist of expanding His kingdom and genuinely caring for people. God puts everyone in our lives for a reason.

During my senior season I was determined that I would be happy for the opportunity that God had given me, regardless of the outcome. That season He blessed me with the best one I had ever had. My twin brother and doubles partner (who was also on the tennis team) only lost 2 NAIA matches and we ended up breaking the school's record for most doubles wins.

But looking back now, I wouldn't have cared if I had lost every single match. All that mattered to me was praying for people and letting my opponents know that Jesus loves them. And that, right there, should always be the desires of your heart.

1. How worldly are your heart's desires?

> "Take delight in The LORD, and he will give you the desires of your heart."
> Psalm 37:4 (NIV)

"I have seen something else under the sun: The race is not to the swift or the battle to the strong, nor does food come to the wise or wealth to the brilliant or favor to the learned; but time and chance happen to them all."

Ecclesiastes 9:11

GAME

52

GRACE BAUGHN

BASKETBALL

UNIVERSITY	PEPPERDINE UNIVERSITY
HOMETOWN	PEACHTREE CORNERS, GEORGIA
JERSEY	#4
POSITION	SHOOTING GAURD
FAVORITE ATHLETE	MISTY MAY AND MATT RYAN
FAVORITE MOVIE	ANY ANIMATED MOVIE
FAVORITE ICE CREAM	MINT CHOCOLATE CHIP
HOBBIES	PLAYING GUITAR AND SINGING
RANDOM FACT	HAS BACK FREEZE WITH BRAIN FREEZE

THE POWER OF WORDS

"Have you heard about his dysfunctional family?"
"She doesn't have any real friends, nobody likes her."
"Did you hear what he did last weekend?"

Do these comments sound familiar? Gossip is everywhere. Think of a time when you heard a rumor about yourself. We have all experienced gossip — whether it was true or not is irrelevant. There is something inside of every person that is deeply affected by the words of others.

Gossip seeks to replace a person's God-given identity by labeling its victim with a new title. When a rumor is true, it degrades the person who is being talked about and causes us as Christians to view a person in light of their sin or failure rather than in the light of God's grace. When a rumor is false, gossip keeps alive a false perception of a person and keeps us from loving our neighbor.

Gossip does not have any place in the body of Christ. The Bible says that the tongue is a double-edged sword. It can build up our brother and sisters in Christ, or it can easily tear them down. Gossip can sneak up so easily in my life, but I try to only say uplifting things. When I find my friends turning to negative talk about someone, I intervene or change the topic. The words from our mouths reveal the state of our hearts. It feels so much better to talk about a person the way God sees them.

1. When are you most prone to gossip about someone?
2. How can you avoid situations that may lead to gossip?

"The words of a gossip are like choice morsels; they go down to a man's inmost parts"
Proverbs 18:8 (NIV)

53

JOSH BRAME

ROWING

UNIVERSITY	BAYLOR UNIVERSITY
HOMETOWN	DALLAS, TEXAS
JERSEY	N/A
POSITION	STYLE: SWEEPING
FAVORITE ATHLETE	AARON CURTIS
FAVORITE MOVIE	HEAT
FAVORITE ICE CREAM	CHOCOLATE CHIP COOKIE DOUGH
HOBBIES	CALL OF DUTY
RANDOM FACT	HAS A STRESS INDUCED HEAD TWITCH

SPIRITUAL AND PHYSICAL FITNESS

The end of our season was fast approaching. I had been working harder than ever in my entire college career; but, what was I going to do afterwards? I decided the best way sustain my fitness and intensity was, ironically enough, natural bodybuilding. I had no idea where to start, but I knew that embarking on this endeavor would not be in vain. The same effort that I had expended and the tools I had utilized in-season could transfer to other activities. I knew that I would have to adhere to a proven system, and dedicate my days to reaching my goal.

The discipline of athletes is immense, and it produces a wondrous product. Is this any different from our spiritual walk? Absolutely not. We are called to go out and make disciples. Here are a few things to read and keep in mind when attempting to do so:

A. Appreciate the uniqueness of the Bible. It is unlike any other book.
   1. Focus on 2 Timothy 3:16 in particular.
   2. The Bible was composed by 40 authors across 1500 years and in 3 languages. The one theme is "redemption of the world" via Jesus.

B. Commit to soaking up scripture, concentrating on tackling smaller sections.
   1. Do you every try to read a big chunk of the Bible at a time? You are missing out on many intricate details!
   2. Reread the first verses of Genesis slowly and make new observations.

C. Determine to listen and follow God's commands.
   1. It is not just about finding and memorizing the good news, it is about application, and living and presenting it to others.

The same way we train for our matches, regattas, tournaments, or big games, we need to train for our spirituality. We never know when God may call us to disciple one of His children!

1. Am I spiritually fit right now, or do I need to take steps to prepare for the "big game"?

"No discipline seems pleasant at the time, but painful. Later on, however, it produces a harvest of righteousness and peace for those who have been trained by it."
Hebrews 12:11 (NIV)

54

KEVIN WASHINGTON

FOOTBALL

UNIVERSITY NOTRE DAME AND ABILENE CHRISTIAN

HOMETOWN  SUGAR LAND, TEXAS

JERSEY #42 AND #55

POSITION  LINEBACKER

FAVORITE ATHLETE  JERRY RICE AND MIKE SINGLETARY

FAVORITE MOVIE  BOOK OF ELI

FAVORITE ICE CREAM  THE GREAT DIVIDE

HOBBIES  READING AND TIME WITH WIFEY

RANDOM FACT  WORKED FOR MUHAMMAD ALI

S-IN-FECTION

It never starts off as a big deal — maybe a cut or a sore that is not taken care of properly. But if we are not careful, something small can lead to something as radical as an amputation.

Think about this scenario: someone walking around hunched over, aching bones, depressed, dull eyes, lonely and anxious. These symptoms describe sin taking a physical toll on King David. In Psalm 38, he cries out to God and describes his pain.

Often times, we think that sin only affects us emotionally. For those in true relationship with Christ, however, it affects everything. We can feel the separation from the Lord of Glory and from the Savior whose loving sacrifice we have dishonored. What is even scarier though, is the road that leads us there.

The Bible tells us sin is deceitful and therefore sneakily slides into our lives. What starts off as little things become bigger over time, eventually hardening us to the point of not even noticing something is wrong. What's worse is that as sin continues to grow in or around us, it makes us seek it out more and more. The question is, what do we do about it? Well, you do what athletes do. You train.

Athletes watch film, practice and workout, all in an effort to strengthen weaknesses; to know the enemy and overcome deficiencies. Christians are called to do the same through the power of Christ's sacrifice. A good athlete takes care of the little things to be as effective as possible and Christians should do likewise. Then we will be killing sin, instead of sin killing us.

1. Philippians 4:6-9 gives us a training regimen if you will. Pray. Think. Act. Pray that God would strengthen you. Think biblically about situations or people. Act according to what you know you should do. How can you apply this?

"But encourage one another other daily, as long as it is called "Today," so that none of you may be hardened by sin's deceitfulness."
Hebrews 3:13 (NIV)

55

JACK EAST

LACROSSE

UNIVERSITY	PALM BEACH ATLANTIC UNIVERSITY
HOMETOWN	NEW ORLEANS, LOUISIANA
JERSEY	#11
POSITION	MIDFIELD AND LSM
FAVORITE ATHLETE	THE UGANDA NATIONAL LACROSSE TEAM
FAVORITE MOVIE	GLADIATOR
FAVORITE ICE CREAM	VANILLA WITH GUMMY BEARS
HOBBIES	LEADING WORSHIP
RANDOM FACT	BEAT GUITAR HERO II ON EXPERT

CONSIDER IT PURE JOY

What brings you pure joy? Not just a temporary happiness, but pure and lasting joy? For most of us, trials and struggles are likely not the first things to spring to the forefront of our minds. When we are faced with trials and difficulties, and our faith is tested, is it possible to view these trials as a gift from God?

It was my first season playing lacrosse in college, and the third day of practice. We were doing a simple one-on-one drill. When I went to cut, I felt my ankle turn and heard a crunch that I will never forget. Not only had I managed to break my own ankle, but I also dislocated it and tore some ligaments as well. It was not a great sight for all those around. I laid there in shock, and we waited for the ambulance. As they were getting me ready to move, I remember in a slight daze asking one of the paramedics how long I'd be out for, to which he replied, "Sorry kid, your season is over."

As athletes, we come across trials and adversity constantly. Maybe like me, you have struggled with a serious injury, fighting for a position, or the day-to-day grind of practice and preparation on top of what seems like endless amounts of school work. When it comes to sports, new challenges can appear at any time. How do we consider these things pure joy?

God allows us to go through these trials because He ultimately knows the value they bring to our lives. In the words of Charles Spurgeon, "If God so wills: the worst calamity is the wisest and kindest thing that could befall to me if God ordains it. We know that all things work together for good to them that love God." I am constantly struck by these words. If it is in God's plan, then what I may deem to be the worst thing possible is the best thing that could have happened. Sometimes it just takes us a little time to come to this realization.

When I suffered the ankle injury, I had no idea that two years later I would transfer to a small Christian University in south Florida, or that two years later I would prepare for my senior season with a strong chance of competing for a National Championship. The injury granted me one more season, and allowed me the opportunity to be part of something special. None of this would be possible if I had used that year of eligibility. In our trials, we can take refuge in the fact that God ultimately has our best interest at heart, and He knows what is best for us. This is what allows me to face the trials I come across, with pure joy.

1. What does it look like for you to consider it pure joy when you face your current trials?

"Consider it pure joy, my brothers and sisters, whenever you face trials of many kinds."
James 1:2 (NIV)

56

MOLLY COPPADGE

SOCCER

UNIVERSITY	TABOR COLLEGE
HOMETOWN	CHARLOTTE, NORTH CAROLINA
JERSEY	#17
POSITION	MIDFIELDER
FAVORITE ATHLETE	MIA HAMM
FAVORITE MOVIE	THE SANDLOT
FAVORITE ICE CREAM	CHOCOLATE
HOBBIES	CRAFTING AND SHOPPING
RANDOM FACT	HAS LIVED IN 5 DIFFERENT STATES

IDENTIFYING OUR GIFTS

I started my collegiate career at a junior college that was nationally known for its soccer program. After my freshman season, Coach called me in for my individual meeting. He quickly informed me that I was not getting my spot back on the roster for the next year. Skills–wise, I was at the bottom of the team and he needed to fill my spot with someone more talented. He asked if I would be the team manager for the following season.

How embarrassing that was for me. First, I got recruited to play college soccer, then discovered I was not good enough for the team. Then my coach asked me to be the team's manager. I had no clue how I was going to tell my friends and family that my playing days were over. However, I agreed to be the manager for the following season.

Hardly any appreciation was given for everything that I and the other managers did for the athletes that season. I mean, who wants to wash dirty, smelly soccer uniforms and practice gear? Or have a coach and players barking orders at you, rarely saying "please" or "thank you"? Not many people I know. But through this experience, I was able to identify a gift God so graciously gave me: my willingness to serve others regardless of what I received back.

Often, we think we have all our gifts and talents figured out. Yet, sometimes it takes going through a trying time to realize that we have more gifts beyond the ability to play a sport. I was convinced that God gave me the gift of athleticism. However, I did not know that He would turn that into the gift of a servant heart.

I survived the season as a team manager. My coach even helped me get recruited to a four year private college to finish out my playing career despite not playing for a season. After that experience at junior college, I do not take anything for granted. I look for different ways to serve others with the talents and abilities that were given to me from God.

1. Besides having the talent to play a college sport, what other gifts has God given you?

"Each of you should use whatever gifts you have received to serve others, as faithful stewards of God's grace in its various forms."
1 Peter 4:10 (NIV)

57

ETHAN JAEGER

BASEBALL

UNIVERSITY	TRUMAN STATE UNIVERSITY
HOMETOWN	EUREKA, MISSOURI
JERSEY	#21
POSITION	PITCHER AND FIRST BASEMAN
FAVORITE ATHLETE	CHRIS PAUL
FAVORITE MOVIE	A TIME TO KILL
FAVORITE ICE CREAM 	WHITE CHOCOLATE MOUSSE
HOBBIES	DANCING, FISHING, MARIO KART N64
RANDOM FACT 	KENTUCKY BORN - CLAIMS SOUTHERN ROOTS

FOLLOW THE LEADER

We have all had those practices and games where the entire team blows it. Coach's reply: "To the foul pole (or your sport's respective starting line for commencement of punishment)."

I remember one practice specifically when I was a junior on Truman State's baseball team. About an hour into practice, we started running and then ran sprints for two and a half hours. As a pitcher, I took pride in my conditioning. I was in great shape, so the running didn't faze me too much. But it was definitely frustrating to run for others' mistakes. The sun went down and about a half hour later Coach called it.

Everyone was leaving when he pulled me aside and challenged me: "E, you work your butt off and you push yourself harder than I can push you. I'll never question that. But, I need to you be a leader on this team and push the other guys. They'll follow you."

Up to this point, I had never led. I always stood alone and worried about myself and my performance. The challenge to lead came as a shock, but I took Coach seriously. I decided to take a leadership role on the team. I had no idea where to start, so I asked God to teach me. He led me to the book of Exodus.

God called Moses to lead His people out of bondage and oppression in Egypt. But Moses threw God every excuse for why he couldn't do it. "Who will I say has sent me?" Moses asked. God instructed him to say, "I AM has sent me." "What if they don't believe that You sent me?" he asked. God gave Moses a staff, and a blood-red Nile as miraculous signs. Moses claimed to be without eloquence and slow of speech and tongue. God provided Aaron to speak on Moses' behalf. After all of this, Moses STILL had the audacity to ask God to send someone else. But God refused and used Moses to change the world.

God calls upon each of us to be leaders. As followers of Christ, it is our privilege to lead others to Him. By reading about Moses, I discovered that leadership requires reliance on God's strength. I was not prepared to lead anyone, but God used me to reach some of my teammates in a way I will never forget. God wants to use you, too, in everything you do. Just like Moses, God will give you everything you need to impact those around you, and you will be amazed at how He changes you in the process.

1. How can you challenge yourself so that those around you are forced to see Jesus living through you?

Exodus 3 and 4

58

KIRK BRYANT

FOOTBALL

UNIVERSITY — MISSISSIPPI COLLEGE

HOMETOWN — LUBBOCK, TEXAS

JERSEY — #11

POSITION — WIDE RECEIVER

FAVORITE ATHLETE — DANNY AMENDOLA

FAVORITE MOVIE — HUNGER GAMES

FAVORITE ICE CREAM — ROCKY ROAD

HOBBIES — SKIING

RANDOM FACT — CAN JUGGLE KNIVES

GIVING THANKS

Whether it is concussions, broken bones, or torn ligaments, athletes understand that there is a risk to the sport that they love to play. Football is no different. Injuries do occur, and they are tough to overcome in such a physical sport.

I have firsthand knowledge of this because I am currently taking a medical redshirt for a foot injury that I suffered during spring football practice.

Paul writes in his first letter to the Thessalonians in chapter 5, verse 18; "give thanks in all circumstances, for this is God's will for you in Christ Jesus." As frustrating as it is, I realize that God's will and His plans are perfect.

In 1 Peter 5:10 it says, "And the God of all grace, who called you to His eternal glory in Christ, after you have suffered a little while, will Himself restore you and make you strong, firm, and steadfast." God also promises is James 1:12 to bless those who persevere under many trials.

As athletes, this is what we need. We are always exhausted and pushing hard, but the satisfaction of winning drives us. How amazing is it that we know that God will restore us and that we win? If you ask me, that's pretty exciting. Be encouraged and thankful for how much He blesses us each and every day.

1. Today, how can you show how thankful you are for what Christ has done in your life?
2. What are some small things in your life that need an eternal perspective?

"Rejoice always, pray continually, give thanks in all circumstances; for this is God's will for you in Christ Jesus."

1 Thessalonians 5:16-18 (NIV)

59

MATT GALVIN

CROSS-COUNTRY - TRACK

UNIVERSITY	BAYLOR UNIVERSITY
HOMETOWN	DALLAS, TEXAS
JERSEY	N/A
POSITION	N/A
FAVORITE ATHLETE	ERIC LIDDELL
FAVORITE MOVIE	BRAVEHEART
FAVORITE ICE CREAM	CHOCOLATE CHIP
HOBBIES	WORKING AT KANAKUK
RANDOM FACT	CAN BLOW BUBBLEGUM 2 FEET WIDE

SPIRITUAL ENDURANCE

When I think of endurance, I think of a race. When I first started running, I wanted to burst from the line and use all of my energy in the first lap. I soon learned how to pace myself after not having enough energy or endurance to last the whole race.

Racing also gets tiring. There is a point in the race where all runners "hit the wall," or start to tire significantly. A choice has to be made: should the runner go or not go? This is what separates the best runners from the rest. They are the ones that make the move and press forward, even when they do not think their bodies can handle any more.

Racing can be a lot like our spiritual lives. We can get easily fired up by a message or some inspiration which will keep us going for a few days, but does it last?

Part of the tough job we have as Christians is to have endurance, to keep running after Christ no matter what, day after day. We often can hit trials or roadblocks, much like "hitting the wall" during a race. Again, the decision comes: Are we going to give up or are we going to continue to press on and follow after Christ?

I think the definition for Christian endurance should be this: continuing to follow Christ, even when it is hard. Like Hebrews 12:1-2 says, if we fix our eyes on Jesus while we press on during life or whatever "race" we are called to, we will endure because Jesus will carry us through. What a great promise.

Endurance is not easy, but it is worth it. One of the best things about racing is the feeling of satisfaction that you get from finishing a race. It is one of the greatest feelings in the world.

An even greater feeling will be the one that we will receive from God in heaven when we complete our earthly race. I can only imagine Jesus telling us, "Well done, my good and faithful servant!" This is why we are called to endure: so that we can finish the race well, and ultimately glorify God.

1. How can you build a spiritual endurance that will keep you going during hard times?

"Therefore, since we are surrounded by such a great cloud of witnesses, let us throw off everything that hinders and the sin that so easily entangles. And let us run with perseverance the race marked out for us, fixing our eyes on Jesus, the pioneer and perfecter of faith. For the joy set before him he endured the cross, scorning its shame, and sat down at the right hand of the throne of God."

Hebrews 12:1-2 (NIV)

60

KELSEY DUNAWAY

VOLLEYBALL

UNIVERSITY	XAVIER UNIVERSITY
HOMETOWN	LOUISVILLE, KENTUCKY
JERSEY	#9
POSITION	OUTSIDE HITTER
FAVORITE ATHLETE	JACKIE ROBINSON
FAVORITE MOVIE	FRIDAY NIGHT LIGHTS
FAVORITE ICE CREAM	COOKIE DOUGH
HOBBIES	BAKING AND TRAVELING
RANDOM FACT	MET MIKE POSNER TWICE

YOU ARE ADEQUATE

At the end of my junior year. I tore the labrum in my hitting shoulder. I rehabbed my shoulder for months, getting it ready for my senior year. The second week of preseason, I dislocated my shoulder again, putting my volleyball career in a terrible position. My shoulder was not strong enough to hit at a D1 competition level, and the season was just starting. There was no time to get it healed and ready in time for games to start.

I was crushed. I had been playing competitive volleyball for 16 years, and it was all I knew. I remember a few days after I dislocated my shoulder, I cried to my coach. I told him that I wasn't good enough to do anything else with my life, and that I was lost without my volleyball talent. I felt inadequate not being the star volleyball player.

Then, I reached out to God. He reminded me that I am His child and that I was created in His image. By reading God's word in the Bible, I realized my new mission. It was time for me to push my teammates in practice, to give them advice on how to play better and to support them from the bench. I learned to be selfless. I realized that I was adequate and that God had something greater planned for my life. I learned that volleyball isn't everything, but that living out God's word is. Follow God's word, and he will provide something better for your life then you would ever have imagined.

1. Do you believe you are adequate enough in your sport and in God's love?

"Such confidence we have through Christ before God. Not that we are competent in ourselves to claim anything for ourselves, but our competence comes from God. He has made us competent as ministers of a new covenant—not of the letter but of the spirit; for the letter kills, but the spirit gives life."

2 Corinthians 3:4-6 (NIV)

61

EMMA PAPPENFUSS

CHEER

UNIVERSITY	SOUTHERN ILLINOIS UNIVERSITY
HOMETOWN	HARRISBURG, ILLINOIS
JERSEY	N/A
POSITION	FLYER
FAVORITE ATHLETE	SHAWN JOHNSON AND LEBRON JAMES
FAVORITE MOVIE	OBSESSED WITH HUNGER GAMES
FAVORITE ICE CREAM	ANYTHING CHOCOLATE
HOBBIES	PHOTOGRAPHY, EATING WITH FRIENDS, PIANO
RANDOM FACT	STARTED DRINKING COFFEE IN COLLEGE

THE PARTY? WHAT PARTY?

As far as athletics go, the transition from high school to college cheerleading was like nothing I had ever experienced. I had gone from cheering with my best friends my whole life to being suddenly thrown into a group of girls who I had never met. It did not help that I am the shy, quiet type, one who typically does not draw a crowd.

After a few weeks, I started to notice some of the girls had a lot in common, things that I simply did not. I watched as they formed bonds...without me. At the beginning of the year they would invite me, but I would always decline. I knew most of them were not Christians and they just assumed I did not party. They were always friendly and genuine, but I allowed Satan to convince me that I was not good enough to be on the team, and that I did not belong.

Then one day, the youth pastor from my church sent out a routine group text message. I nearly dismissed it, but something about it caught my eye. I had noticed that his signature was Galatians 1:10, "For am I now seeking the approval of man, or of God? Or am I trying to please man? If I were still trying to please man, I would not be a servant of Christ."

That is when I realized that I longed for their approval, and I had become dejected when I realized that garnering it would mean compromising my Christian values. I eventually came to terms with this and came to know that my life should be a constant act of worship, bringing glory to God. If I am in it to please man, it would be impossible for me to do so; for we are human and full of faults, and are therefore never truly satisfied when focusing on that which is outside of the domain of our Lord and Savior.

Jesus calls us the salt of the earth and the light of the world, and looking back, I take joy in being different for Christ's sake.

1. Can your teammates tell that you live for Christ, or do you blend in with the rest of the world?

"Am I trying to win the approval of human beings, or of God? Or am I trying to please people? If I were trying to please people, I would not be a servant of Christ."
Galatians 1:10 (NIV)

62

LEE TENENOFF

FOOTBALL

UNIVERSITY	BETHEL COLLEGE
HOMETOWN	PANAMA CITY, PANAMA
JERSEY	#15
POSITION	LINEBACKER
FAVORITE ATHLETE	RAY LEWIS
FAVORITE MOVIE	GLADIATOR
FAVORITE ICE CREAM	CHOCOLATE BROWNIE
HOBBIES	HUNTING, FISHING, WORKING OUT
RANDOM FACT	BLIND IN LEFT EYE

JOY IN LOVE

I have never been an incredible athlete. I did not play on a varsity team till my senior year of high school. When I expressed my desire to play college football, my high school head coach told me I was "too small" and "too slow" to make it on the field. College football was a dream of mine and I wanted to make it happen.

I ended up walking into a school that was not even close to my first choice. The football team was not good and the coaching staff was not the type of men I wanted to be coached by. Through this whole process, my identity was wrapped up in football and my discouragement from not making the travel team reflected it.

At the end of my freshman year, I transferred to Bethel University in Minnesota. The coaches cared about me and the guys on the team were the best. During my sophomore year, I tore my ACL during the sixth game of the season.

After being at Bethel for a while, I thought my identity was in Christ rather than football. By tearing my ACL it became clear to me that my identity was still too wrapped up in football and lifting.

When I returned to the field the next year, I realized tearing my ACL was the best thing that could have happened to encourage and evaluate my walk with the Lord. I made the travel squad my junior year and played on all the special teams but still wanted more from football. I found myself asking God why he gave me such a passion for football and then did not make me a freak athlete. I'm sure every Christian athlete has asked this at some point during their career.

God showed me that if all I had was being good at football I would never be happy or fulfilled. No matter what role I am in or how much playing time I get, it is not about how much I am encouraged, recognized, exalted, respected, or loved. Our calling is to love, encourage, and respect others and let the rest take care of itself. Looking somewhere besides Christ for fulfillment is setting us up for disappointment.

When I think about who Jesus would have been on a football team, I don't see him as the starting quarterback leading the team to victory, I don't see Him as a middle linebacker knocking people out and demanding respect. I see Him as the guy on the team that loves and serves everyone around, the guy that lives His life and plays his sport to the best of his ability each and every day of his life.

1. Are you trusting God with your current situation where he has you in life?

"This is how we know what love is: Jesus Christ laid down his life for us. And we ought to lay down our lives for our brothers and sisters."
1 John 3:16 (NIV)

63

LOGAN LOWERY

BASKETBALL

UNIVERSITY	BAYLOR UNIVERSITY
HOMETOWN	KINGWOOD, TEXAS
JERSEY	#20
POSITION	FORWARD
FAVORITE ATHLETE	LEBRON JAMES
FAVORITE MOVIE	FORREST GUMP
FAVORITE ICE CREAM	BLUE BELL VANILLA
HOBBIES 	DUCK/DOVE HUNTING, VIDEO GAMES
RANDOM FACT 	BEEN TO 30 STATES AND 3 COUNTRIES

PREPARING FOR BATTLE

As a student athlete at a NCAA Division I university, I have learned all too well what it means to prepare. At Baylor, our basketball coaches always tell us "every battle is won before it's fought." The point they are trying to make is that the days of preparation leading up to our "battle," or game, are going to determine how we perform when tested on the court. The game is merely a reflection of how well we prepared. Figuratively speaking, our team is the horse that must be prepared for its day of battle.

I think in many ways my personal life is like a basketball game when it comes to preparation and battles. There are multiple battles that I face each day , whether it is sin, temptation, pride, a bad day at practice or a poor grade on an exam. We all have different battles and each one presents the opportunity to respond in a positive or negative way. Proverbs 21:31 reminds us that in order to be victorious over our personal battles, we must prepare for them ahead of time.

What does preparing for a personal battle mean? I like to think about the possible battles that lie ahead. When I do so, I am able to think about how I can avoid the situation completely, or how I can respond in a way that is pleasing to the Lord. Preparing for battle also means that I must stay rooted in Christian values by reading His word and spending time in prayer. Of course we all make mistakes and lose battles from time to time, but preparing for them increases our chances of winning.

It is also very important to not overlook the second part of Proverbs 21:31, which tells us that victory belongs to the Lord. The verse indicates that it is our responsibility to prepare for the battles before us, but ultimately God is sovereign and any battle we win, whether in life or sports, is because He so graciously allowed for it to happen. By doing so, God gives us a wonderful opportunity to give Him all the praise and glory.

Let us take the time to prepare for our daily battles so that we may overcome them and praise the Lord!

1. How can you prepare ahead of time for your personal battles so that you might overcome them when challenged?

"The horse is made ready for the day of battle, but victory rests with the LORD."
Proverbs 21:31 (NIV)

64

MARY BURKE

GYMNASTICS

UNIVERSITY: UNIVERSITY OF MISSOURI

HOMETOWN: PALATINE, ILLINOIS

JERSEY: N/A

POSITION: EVENT: ALL AROUND

FAVORITE ATHLETE: DOMINIQUE DAWES AND MICHAEL JORDAN

FAVORITE MOVIE: THE SANDLOT

FAVORITE ICE CREAM: MOOSE TRACKS

HOBBIES: RUNNING, HIKING, MOVIES

RANDOM FACT: WORE PIGTAILS EVERYDAY AS A KID

GOD'S PLAN FOR US

I have heard Romans 8:28 many times throughout my life. I did not realize the full meaning of it, however, until a career-threatening injury put my faith to the test.

As a gymnast, injuries are nothing new to me, but when I fractured my shin during my sophomore season I was devastated. Sitting and watching my team practice and not being able to contribute was one of the hardest things I have ever experienced. At the peak of my career, I did not understand why this happened, and I could not accept that this was actually part of God's plan for me. At a time when I needed to trust God the most, I found that I was distancing myself from Him. I thought if God really is working for my good, doesn't He want me to succeed in my sport?

It was not until a friend reintroduced this scripture to me and challenged me to look deeper into this verse that I understood the significance of it. God promises that He is always working for our good, but He also states that it is according to His purpose.

At that moment I realized that I had been living for my own desires, not according to God's. Although this experience was one of the biggest challenges in my athletic career, I finally understood that there was a reason for it.

Looking back on this injury, as hard as it was for me, I am able to see how much closer it brought me to God and His word. When I stopped trying to understand why this obstacle was placed in my life, I started drawing closer to God and developed a deeper relationship with Him. I have learned that God really does have our best interest in mind and that every difficulty that is placed in our life has a purpose. This experience has taught me to praise God whatever the situation and know that His plan is far greater than my own will.

Trusting in the Lord is a challenge because it forces us to give up control of our lives and put our complete faith in His plan for us. But when we do, we discover that no matter what trials or hardships we are going through, God is not doing it to us, but rather for us. He is doing it to make us stronger, for us to grow in our faith and for us to learn that we need Jesus in everything we do.

Therefore, be thankful for every trial you face. You will discover that living according to God's purpose guarantees you will be taken care of and given the strength to overcome any obstacle you face.

1. In what areas of your life can you trust God better?

"And we know that in all things God works for the good of those who love Him, who have been called according to His purpose."
Romans 8:28 (NIV)

65

MORGAN ROCKWELL

SOCCER

UNIVERSITY	LOUISIANA TECH UNIVERSITY
HOMETOWN	SALT LAKE CITY, UTAH
JERSEY	#2
POSITION	CENTER DEFENDER AND MIDFIELDER
FAVORITE ATHLETE	ALI KRIEGER AND PETR CECH
FAVORITE MOVIE	GREASE
FAVORITE ICE CREAM	COOKIES 'N CREAM
HOBBIES	WORKING OUT
RANDOM FACT	SELF TAUGHT UNICYCLE ENTHUSIAST

GET UP, LIFT UP

Being a member of a team has been one of the most rewarding and influential experiences in my life. My teammates, coaches, and trainers are all crucial when it comes to the delicate balance of building a successful team. The destruction caused by this same dynamic being unbalanced became a recurring issue throughout my college career.

Moving across the country to play soccer was the most exciting and anxiety–filled time of my life. I was moving 1,700 miles away from my family to follow my dreams and immerse myself in a completely new culture. Within the first few weeks, I was introduced to the emotional roller coaster that accompanies the physical and mental burdens of playing a college sport with teammates I had just met a coach whose livelihood rests on our performance.

The countless hours spent working together bonded us into a family in no time at all. Like any family, these are the people expected to be there to build you up and instill confidence, and a lot of the time, this is exactly what happened. However, when things started to go downhill during a season, some would begin to discourage and act selfishly. The season only turned around when we rallied together in spite of the negative aura surrounding the team.

My freshman year of college I gave my life to Christ and joined a whole new team. I realized quickly how important it is to be surrounded by fellow believers who will be there for encouragement and accountability. Living a life for Christ is followed closely by opposition and lack of understanding from non–believers, including friends.

Just as with an athletic team, staying positive and focused can be hard to do when those who are supposed to contributing to the support system are the ones doing the damage. We are made stronger in our pursuit of the Lord when we have fellowship with other believers, both sides pick each other up. We are not called to judge, but to be a part of a family who shows compassion and love for others just as Jesus did, believer or not.

1. Are you following Christ's example and showing love and compassion to those around you?

"Therefore encourage one another and build each other up, just as in fact you are doing."

1 Thessalonians 5:11 (NIV)

66

LEVI NORWOOD

FOOTBALL

UNIVERSITY	BAYLOR UNIVERSITY
HOMETOWN	STATE COLLEGE, PENNSYLVANIA
JERSEY	#42
POSITION	WIDE RECEIVER
FAVORITE ATHLETE	GABE AND JORDAN NORWOOD
FAVORITE MOVIE	THE SANDLOT
FAVORITE ICE CREAM	RITA'S ITALIAN ICE
HOBBIES	PHOTOGRAPHY AND BASKETBALL
RANDOM FACT	STARTED BAYLORS CHAPTER OF UPLIFTING ATHLETES TO SUPPORT CEREBRAL PALSY

MAKE THE TIME SO WE ALL CAN MAKE IT

It goes without saying that college was a hectic time for me. Between my studies and football practices, games and obligations, I was also doing everything that I could to put myself in a favorable position to play in the NFL.

Most people, upon seeing everything I am juggling, would be prone to think, "How does he do it all? He certainly does not have time for anything else."

While I'll concede that my schedule was difficult to juggle, I've always taken a lot of stock in the old adage, "You're never too busy for the things that are most important to you. If it means a lot to you, you'll make time for it."

I am no different. That is how I still found time to help and love God's children. I was on the Fellowship of Christian Athletes leadership board at Baylor and we embarked on mission trips during the summers to share both the Gospel and our love of sports with those who are likely not familiar with either: children, adults, and prisoners in Zambia and Kenya. We also strived to make a difference here at home by visiting schools and sharing how our faith has influenced not only our athletic careers, but our lives as a whole. So get out there. Give back. Because if it's all about what's important, God should win that contest hands down, every single time

1. How is God calling you to give back to His Kingdom?

"In the same way, let your light shine before others, that they may see your good deeds and glorify your Father in heaven."
Matthew 5:16 (NIV)

67

KYLE MCCLELLAN

BASEBALL

UNIVERSITY  DRAFTED OUT OF HIGH SCHOOL

HOMETOWN  FLORISSANT, MISSOURI

JERSEY  #46

POSITION  FORMER STL CARDINALS PITCHER

FAVORITE ATHLETE  BRETT FAVRE

FAVORITE MOVIE  DRURY OUTDOORS SHOW

FAVORITE ICE CREAM  COOKIES 'N CREAM

HOBBIES HUNTING

RANDOM FACT  3.79 EARNED RUN AVERAGE

GO TELL IT

In my 30 years of life, I have heard many a myth and falsehood regarding Christianity. One of the misconceptions I have heard the most is that you need to make a career out of spreading the Gospel. That you have to be a pastor or a missionary in order to bring God's lost children back to Him. This simply is not the case. We all can be a light, no matter what our daily activities and routines entail. We are called to, as Mark 15:16 illustrates.

My only season with the Texas Rangers was an injury-plagued one. I found myself pitching for one of the team's minor-league clubs on rehab assignment. During this stint, I often went to chapel and I made it a point to note who I recognized there from the team. Then I paid attention to their daily interactions with the team. I eventually approached them, posing this simple question: "If Jesus was your locker mate, would He know that you are a believer?" I said they need not answer at the moment, but rather for them to take a night to look in the mirror and think it over.

The next day we reconvened. Not a single "yes" among the group. From this point on, we started meeting for Bible studies. At the beginning, one of the guys could not even tell the difference between the Old Testament and the New, but before long we were baptizing one of the guys in the outfield pool. All just by sharing the faith at a Starbucks. Lives were changed, people were saved, and folks came to know the Lord.

We should never cease to spread the Good News, even upon retirement. Since being out of the Major Leagues, my wife and I have started "Brace for Impact", a foundation that will raise money to help support Haiti orphanages. Our good works will never stop. Every person that we bring to Jesus is one child closer to returning all of his children home to Him.

1. If Jesus was your locker-mate, would He know that you're a believer?

"He said to them, "Go into all the world and preach the gospel to all creation."
Mark 16:15 (NIV)

68

MIKAILA DAVIS

TRACK AND FIELD

UNIVERSITY		CONCORDIA UNIVERSITY-IRVINE
HOMETOWN		SANTA MARIA, CALIFORNIA
JERSEY		N/A
POSITION	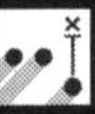	EVENT: SHOT PUT AND DISCUS
FAVORITE ATHLETE		PEYTON MANNING AND TIM TEBOW
FAVORITE MOVIE		THE VOW
FAVORITE ICE CREAM		COOKIE DOUGH
HOBBIES		HANGING AT THE BEACH, HIKING
RANDOM FACT		HOMESCHOOLED UNTIL FRESHMAN YEAR

FAITH THROUGH CHANGE

Instant. That is the only way to describe how my love of basketball came about, back all the way in the 8th grade. I used to say that basketball was the air to my lungs. I felt so unstoppable, and in my small city of Santa Maria, California it was inevitable (at least in my mind) that it would not be long before I was the talk of the town.

But God's plan differed greatly, in the form of a sport that, to be quite honest, I did not know much about; track and field. The switch came my junior year of high school and by the time I embarked on my freshman year in college, it had completely taken over. All the while I was fighting the transition, doing anything and everything to keep God's blessing directly on my basketball career instead.

Freshman year came and went, and knee surgery kept me out of basketball. Needless to say, I was devastated but even more determined to bounce back and prove myself the next year, recapturing the self worth that I felt I had lost. But the new year also brought with it a new coach, and with that, my days on the team were numbered. He cut me after I had played all summer.

I was beyond crushed. That was it. The end of the line. All my hopes and dreams were finished. Done. Just like that. Or so I thought God was there the whole time and I soon learned that He had greater things for my life, if only I fostered my faith in Him. This took quite a while, but I finally came around.

It was not too long before I secured a track scholarship to Concordia University-Irvine, a private university in Southern California. God, of course, had an answer for the difficult adjustment I was enduring: Athletes in Action. Through this, God showed me my purpose and gave me the courage to be a witness to others. It is this that I am most thankful for, above everything that He has provided for me. God is good, all the time, and all the time, God is good!

1. What are some ways that I can build my faith?

"For it is by grace you have been saved, through faith—and this is not from yourselves, it is the gift of God."
Ephesians 2:8 (NIV)

69

KIM MULLER

TENNIS

UNIVERSITY 	INDIANA WESLEYAN UNIVERSITY
HOMETOWN	NORTH CANTON, OHIO
JERSEY	N/A
POSITION	N/A
FAVORITE ATHLETE	RODGER FEDERER AND SERENA WILLIAMS
FAVORITE MOVIE	CATCHING FIRE
FAVORITE ICE CREAM	COFFEE
HOBBIES 	WORKING OUT
RANDOM FACT	NEVER BEEN STUNG BY A BEE

CURBING THE COMPETITIVE MINDSET

Have you ever felt your whole personality and thought process change once you step foot onto the playing field or court? It is like a light switch inside your brain and it puts you in a competitive mindset that you do not have on a normal basis. Your opponent changes from an ordinary person to a rival that needs to be defeated no matter what it takes.

Tennis can be an extremely personal game. It is just you and the one or two people across the net. When I stepped onto the tennis court, the game sometimes became personal, even if I had never met my opponent before. My competitive mindset sometimes caused me to think less of my opponent as a person and become judgmental or angry towards them, just because I wanted to win. My preconceived notions about my opponent made me think that I should win.

As a long-time tennis player, I realized how unholy this habit was and I learned to curb my competitive mindset. Although there are times that a competitive mindset is necessary in a game situation, if it causes us to think negatively about someone, that is where it goes too far.

These kinds of thoughts happen in life outside athletics as well. You may see someone in the store and judge them automatically by the clothes they are wearing or something you overhear them say. You may even think that you are better than them without even knowing who they are. As Philippians 2:3 reminds us, you should "count others more significant than yourselves." We are all created by the same God who calls us to love one another no matter our differences. Let us learn to curb those competitive mindsets and see others like God does: His beloved children.

1. How can you push aside your preconceived thoughts about an opponent (or person in general) and treat them better than you would want to be treated?

"Do nothing out of selfish ambition or vain conceit. Rather, in humility value others above yourselves."
Philippians 2:3 (NIV)

70

MATT SINGLETARY

FOOTBALL

UNIVERSITY	CALIFORNIA POLYTECHNIC STATE
HOMETOWN	LAKE FOREST, ILLINOIS
JERSEY	#91
POSITION	OUTSIDE LINEBACKER
FAVORITE ATHLETE	RUSSELL WILSON
FAVORITE MOVIE	GLADIATOR
FAVORITE ICE CREAM	HALF BAKED BEN AND JERRY'S
HOBBIES	WORKING OUT AND COOKING
RANDOM FACT	SELF PROCLAIMED MASSIVE NERD

DOUBT

Doubt is one of the best tools that Satan has at his disposal. All he does is plant a little seed of worry, anxiety, or fear, and he has us exactly where he wants us. God says that He knows exactly where we are going, at all times. He will never leave us and we are never out of His reach.

There have been times in my life where I really wondered if God had brought me somewhere just to leave me. In my second season at Baylor University, our entire coaching staff got fired and they brought in new staff. The coaches that brought me in were no longer there. I felt like I was stranded at the place that God brought me. There was a lot of anger and frustration on my account, and I was just mad at God for leaving me to fend for myself, or so I thought.

Later that season, I had the opportunity to transfer schools to Cal Polytechnic State University in San Luis Obispo, California. It was one of the best things that had happened in my life. I got to go to a school that was closer to my family and enjoy playing football again, which I realized did not happen when I was at Baylor. I realized that God had me in the palm of his hand the entire time. I thought He had abandoned me. He was waiting for the perfect time for His plan to work. The God that we serve is all–powerful, and He still cares for each one of His children individually. Never forget how much God loves you.

1. Was there ever a time you doubted God's plans for you? How did you respond?

"For I know the thoughts and plans that I have for you," declares the Lord, "plans to prosper you and not to harm you, plans to give you hope and a future."
Jeremiah 29:11 (NIV)

71

LAUREN FENDER

GOLF

UNIVERSITY	BAYLOR UNIVERSITY
HOMETOWN	LEE'S SUMMIT, MISSOURI
JERSEY	N/A
POSITION	N/A
FAVORITE ATHLETE	BUBBA WATSON AND PHIL MICKELSON
FAVORITE MOVIE	FRIDAY NIGHT LIGHTS
FAVORITE ICE CREAM	CHOCOLATE CUSTARD WITH PB AND BANANAS
HOBBIES	WATER SKIING, SNOW SKIING, WAKE BOARDING
RANDOM FACT 	HAS ONE SHORT FINGER AND ONE SHORT TOE

LETTING GO OF CONTROL

It was a beautiful May day and I had returned home for the summer after completing my freshman year. It was my first day back on the lake. It seemed like a perfect getaway after a week of finals. But the day suddenly turned into my worst nightmare when the unthinkable happened.

I was sitting on the front of the boat when we hit some choppy water. In seconds, I was thrown over the front. I went head first under the boat, and I headed straight for the propeller. Moments later, I felt a sharp cutting feeling and then I lost most feeling in my body. It didn't take long after coming to the surface for me to realize that something was seriously wrong—feeling had not returned to my right arm.

On my ambulance ride to the hospital, all I could think about was how I could have died. I was not as invincible as I had thought. After the initial shock wore off, reality sank in and I began to panic. What if I couldn't use my arm again? I was a left-handed golfer, but my right arm was still necessary.

The paramedics did not have answers to my countless questions about the state of my arm. I kept telling them, "I'm a college golfer. My arm has to work. It has to!" That 45-minute ride to the hospital may have been the longest of my life. Fortunately, the Lord in His grace spared my arm that day. I received over 80 stitches, but miraculously no permanent damage was done.

My perspective changed drastically that day, knowing everything I had worked for all those years could disappear in a matter of seconds. I was completely humbled by my lack of control over my life. I thought I had all my plans for college and beyond worked out. Yet God reminded me that tomorrow is not a guarantee. He reminded me that I am living for something much more important than golf. I realized that even if I never got the chance to swing a club again, I would rejoice because God had given me another day to proclaim His glory.

Thankfully, I did make a full recovery, and continue to play the sport I love. But now, I have a healthier perspective.

1. What would you do if you couldn't play your sport anymore? Would you still want to praise God?

"Show me, Lord, my life's end and the number of my days; let me know how fleeting my life is. You have made my days a mere handbreadth; the span of my years is as nothing before you. Everyone is but a breath, even those who seem secure."

Psalm 39:4-5 (NIV)

72

RAYNER FREDRICK

BASKETBALL

UNIVERSITY	MISSISSIPPI COLLEGE
HOMETOWN	OVERLAND PARK, KANSAS
JERSEY	#44
POSITION	FORWARD
FAVORITE ATHLETE	KEVIN LOVE
FAVORITE MOVIE	LORD OF THE RINGS TRILOGY
FAVORITE ICE CREAM	BEN AND JERRY'S PHISH FOOD
HOBBIES	READING AND LEARNING
RANDOM FACT	HAS LIVED IN 7 DIFFERENT STATES

HOPE DOES NOT DISAPOINT

Five years ago, I was starting my collegiate career as a skinny walk–on at William Jewell College with hopes of earning a scholarship down the road. It was the start of an unbelievable journey of highs and lows that basketball, and more importantly, God, would take me on.

My basketball journey was nothing like I envisioned. It broke my heart and accompanied by family issues, sent me into deep depression. I struggled to understand why God would ever take basketball away, give it back in tremendous fashion and then take it back again. It did not make sense. Now it does.

At my wedding, which was attended by teammates and brothers from throughout the years in Washington, Arizona, Texas, Kansas, Missouri, and Mississippi, Coach Pennell embraced me and whispered something in my ear. He said, "Grand Canyon makes sense now." He was right. God had a plan all along and as Proverbs 16:9 says, I planned my course, God established and determined my steps. He showed me on the journey that I cannot place my trust and identity in things of this world, but rather need to invest in the Kingdom because that is what carries on.

The last five years were filled with trials. Looking back now however, it was all worth it. It was worth it to be there for teammates and for the guys who needed it. To be a leader and team captain, and, hopefully set a precedent for the freshmen who looked up to me.

The struggle led me to the woman of my dreams and prepared me for her. I needed to feel the flames and be molded, shaped, and refined. Those flames brought about perseverance, and truly formed my character which gave me hope. Not hope in the worldly sense, but in the biblical sense—the knowledge that despite what the world says, God will not bail. That is what true hope is. It does not disappoint. Ball is a beautiful thing. But it is not life. Fight the good fight.

1. How will you keep an "even keel" and remain constant despite trials?

"Not only so, but we also glory in our sufferings, because we know that suffering produces perseverance, character; and character, hope. And hope does not put us to shame, because God's love has been poured out into our hearts through the Holy Spirit, who has been given to us."

Romans 5:3-5 (NIV)

73

PAIGE HOLLAND

VOLLEYBALL

UNIVERSITY	STEPHEN F. AUSTIN STATE UNIVERSITY
HOMETOWN	MAGNOLIA, TEXAS
JERSEY	#1
POSITION	SETTER
FAVORITE ATHLETE	MICHAEL JORDAN
FAVORITE MOVIE	MULAN AND YOU'VE GOT MAIL
FAVORITE ICE CREAM	COOKIES 'N CREAM
HOBBIES	GOLF, PING PONG, DRINKING SWEET TEA
RANDOM FACT	LOVES DOING CARTWHEELS

CONSIDER THE BIRDS

It was freshman year, report day, and I was nothing short of terrified. Walking into the locker room, I immediately felt worthless. The girl to the right of me was taller, the one in front was a better server and my teammate across the room was skinnier than me. What characteristics did I have that could compete with all of that and contribute to this team? I truly believed that no one would even notice me. But I was wrong; He more than notices every single one of us.

Have you ever thought of how many birds there are in the world? It seems like there are so many that it would be impossible to count them all. But the Bible tells us that God knows every single one of them! Not one bird is forgotten. If God loves each individual bird so much, is it so unfathomable to comprehend how much He loves each one of us? Psalm 139 tells us that God knows when we sit, when we stand, what we are thinking... everything. He formed each of us by His own hands and knows exactly how many hairs are on our heads. How could we ever feel forsaken or forgotten?

Jesus Christ died for the sins of the entire world. Because of His sacrifice, a relationship with God, the creator of the universe, is possible and we can be called His children.

1. In what ways can you appreciate God for the purposes He has given you?

"Are not five sparrows sold for two pennies? And not one of them is forgotten by God. Indeed, the very hairs of your head are all numbered. Don't be afraid; you are worth more than many sparrows."

Luke 12:6-7 (NIV)

74

MIKE MCNEELY

FOOTBALL

UNIVERSITY UNIVERSITY OF FLORIDA

HOMETOWN CLEARWATER, FLORIDA

JERSEY #31

POSITION RECEIVER

FAVORITE ATHLETE BRETT FAVRE

FAVORITE MOVIE SHREK

FAVORITE ICE CREAM MINT CHOCOLATE CHUNK

HOBBIES PING PONG

RANDOM FACT BEEN TO MORE THAN 30 STATES

YOU ARE ALWAYS LOVED

I grew up in a great home with parents who loved me and wanted the best for me. They valued education and hard work. From an early age, I was taught that if I worked hard enough, I could attain success. Although the idea of hard work and trust in God–given abilities is honorable and important, they became idols in my life that took on an unhealthy and ungodly role, which caused me to develop a broken sense of identity and self–worth. If I was not succeeding, then who was I?

My self–perception was based on my achievements and I believed that by working hard enough, I could be anything and earn others' love and appreciation. Here is the problem with self–worth based on success or talents; what happens when you fail? When things fall apart? When you work as hard as you can, and it doesn't work out? This happened to me both academically and athletically. I was crushed and left questioning who I was.

This is when God revealed Himself to me. He loves us so much that while we were still sinners, He died for us! Before we even knew Him, He loved us. While we were still sinning, He died for us. Even when we fail, He STILL loves us.

You see, we cannot earn God's affection. We will always fall short. That's why Christ came to live the life that we could not and died the death that we deserve. Our faith is counted to us as righteousness. When we fail, the world will turn its back to us (especially in the what-have-you-done-for-me-lately world of sports); but God will always love you. He always has, and He always will. Do not build your house on the sand that will be washed away when the storms of life come. Build it on the rock. Live in the light of Christ's love, and you will be free indeed!

1. Is your self-worth in your accomplishments?
2. Are there areas of your life where you are trying to earn the affection of others?

"Jesus replied, 'Very truly I tell you, everyone who sins is a slave to sin. Now a slave has no permanent place in the family, but a son belongs to it forever. So if the Son sets you free, you will be free indeed.'"

John 8:34-36 (NIV)

75

MATT GIBBS

BASEBALL

UNIVERSITY 	PURDUE UNIVERSITY
HOMETOWN 	COLUMBUS, OHIO
JERSEY	#27
POSITION	PITCHER
FAVORITE ATHLETE	BUBBA WATSON
FAVORITE MOVIE	HOW TO TRAIN YOUR DRAGON
FAVORITE ICE CREAM	MINT CHOCOLATE CHIP
HOBBIES	FLY FISHING, BACKPACKING
RANDOM FACT	REALLY ENJOYS CHEESY SCI-FI MOVIES

BUT IF NOT

Let me start by staging a little background for this verse. If you have not read Daniel yet, switch to that right now, because it is incredible. Then you can come back and read my testimony.

My sophomore year in college, I was riding a spiritual high after a summer of biblical growth like I had never experienced before. At the same time, I was competing for more playing time on the ball field. Throughout the fall and winter, I had been praying that the Lord's will would be done in my life, assuming that His plan for me included on–the–field success so that I would have a greater platform to spread His glory, and at no point did I even consider other options. That assumption turned out to be completely wrong.

I ended up redshirting, which effectively ended my season and wasted months of training. I was absolutely crushed, and started blaming myself, my teammates, my coaches, and even God. Especially God. I thought He had abandoned me, but little did I know that it would be the biggest turning point in my college career.

In my time away from the team, the endeavor of balancing baseball and living for Christ was put into perspective. From that point on, I saw that instead of being a baseball player who is a Christian as long as things went according to my plan, I am eternally a servant of Christ on my team, regardless of what happens, even when my plan doesn't match His.

Baseball was my idol no more, and my prayers changed from, "Do this for me God", to "Lord, please let me succeed in what I am doing, but if not, I know that You have a plan for me."

Having the faith to say "but if not" to God, and accepting different outcomes with grace will let you experience the full power of God's perfect plan for your life. As hard as those different outcomes may be, ultimately if you decide to use them for God's glory, you will begin to see how He works in your life.

1. Is it your intention to succeed merely for your own satisfaction or rather for God's glory?

"If we are thrown into the blazing furnace, the God we serve is able to deliver us from it, and He will deliver us from Your Majesty's hand. But even if He does not, we want you to know, Your Majesty, that we will not serve your gods or worship the image of gold you have set up."

Daniel 3:17-18 (NIV)

76

LAUREN REEDY

SWIMMING

UNIVERSITY UNIVERSITY OF MISSOURI

HOMETOWN ROCHESTER HILLS, MISSISSIPPI

JERSEY N/A

POSITION EVENT: 1M, 3M, AND PLATFORM

FAVORITE ATHLETE CALVIN JOHNSON AND DAVID BOOTH

FAVORITE MOVIE REMEMBER THE TITANS

FAVORITE ICE CREAM ALL OF THEM

HOBBIES ANYTHING ACTIVE AND PLAYING WITH KIDS

RANDOM FACT IRONICALLY AFRAID OF HEIGHTS

TRAINING IN GODLINESS

I had it memorized. It was even on the back of my favorite t–shirt. I had clearly observed the verse, but for the longest time I had totally failed to apply it to my life.

As athletes, we do a lot of things to train for our sport. You probably practice multiple days per week, or maybe multiple times in one day! You are probably careful to properly nourish your body. You probably lift weights or run, or do both. You probably communicate with and have meetings with your coach. All of those things are probably high priorities in your life. You probably schedule all other things around those things. You probably don't often skip those essential pieces of you training. If you did, you probably wouldn't see anything better than mediocre results.

Those things are all very important to getting top notch results in your sport, but those are all examples of physical training. Those are only of some value, but godliness has value in all things. And just as you train in your sport, you must train in godliness as well.

I find it very easy to get this backward. For example, when I go a full day without practicing or doing cardio, or doing something physically active, I feel like a bum, like I just completely wasted a day; but when I go a full day without quiet time or some intentional time in prayer, I am not nearly as upset. I would drop just about everything to be at practice and be fully focused on what I am doing, but I don't fight nearly as hard for my quiet time. Or how about the fact that I wouldn't dream of texting or checking Facebook while in the middle of a meeting with my coach, but somehow I think that's okay when I'm spending time talking to and listening to God? Or when Satan gets in my mind and prevents me from having a good practice, I am furious; but when he prevents me from having a solid quiet time, it doesn't seem to bother me.

If godliness has more value than physical training, then the same level of intensity and commitment I apply to physical training for my sport should be applied to my training in godliness. My quiet time, my prayer time, my FCA weekly meetings, my small group meetings should be held just as sacred as my practice time, lifting time, and meetings with my coaches.

1. Are there any examples of how you may have 1 Timothy 4:8 backwards?

"For physical training is of some value, but godliness has value for all things, holding promise for both the present life and the life to come."
1 Timothy 4:8 (NIV)

“I have fought the good fight, I have finished the race, I have kept the faith.”

1 Timothy 4:7

POST-GAME

77

PATRICK CONE

FOOTBALL

UNIVERSITY	STETSON UNIVERSITY
HOMETOWN	CHATTANOOGA, TENNESSEE
JERSEY	#49
POSITION	MIDDLE LINEBACKER
FAVORITE ATHLETE	JOHN LYNCH
FAVORITE MOVIE	BRAVEHEART
FAVORITE ICE CREAM	CHOCOLATE
HOBBIES	WORKING OUT
RANDOM FACT	LOVES SKIING

PRIDE COMES BEFORE THE FALL

When I arrived at Stetson University, it was exactly one year before the commencement of the Stetson football program. The huge blessing of this decision is that I had the opportunity to get my academic footing under me and train intensely for football.

During that time, the Lord graciously blessed me with a God–fearing man who became my spiritual and physical mentor. Spiritually, he guided me through the loss of my father two years earlier, who tragically committed suicide. Physically, he directed me in the greatest gains of my life. Sounds like the beginning of a great story, right? There is an old saying that originated from Proverbs 16:18, "Pride comes before the fall." Although I began as the starting fullback of Stetson University, and was humbled that God allowed me to be in that position, I finished my football career as a bench–warming linebacker who would never see the football field in the starting lineup ever again.

At first, I was completely aware that God was the only reason I had the opportunity to play college football. I was overwhelmed with how God was taking care of me despite the heartbreaking loss of my father. Yet, when pride creeps into your life, all humility begins to dissipate.

Pride is like a weed in the grass. If you do not kill a weed at its conception, the weed will slowly take over the entire yard. If there are no radical steps to kill the spreading weed, it will eventually choke the grass to death. This slow takeover is exactly what occurred in my heart. In the beginning, the weed was planted when my running back coach greatly upset me with extreme verbal abuse. I did not want to hear the obscene profanity and talked to the head football coach, asking to be switched to middle linebacker. The weed began to spread rapidly as I thought, "Wow, I think I can start as middle linebacker…I am the biggest and fastest of the linebackers…I can become captain of the team…"

Here is the Reader's Digest of the story: I sat the bench until the end of my football career. And PRAISE THE LORD FOR THAT. You see, in my mind, God could have allowed me to start as middle linebacker and allowed all the fame and glory, but He did not. Instead, God saved me from the destruction that eventually follows pride. He rescued me from myself. He picked me up out of an empty pit and allowed me to remain with Him. In the end, God saved me by completely wrecking the yard of my heart, replacing the fatal weed with an all new entity—His richest soil.

1. Are you going to allow God to replace the weed of pride in your life with His rich soil of grace?

"Pride goes before destruction, a haughty spirit before a fall."
Proverbs 16:18 (NIV)

78

MITCH SCHOEN

CROSS-COUNTRY - TRACK

UNIVERSITY	WHEATON COLLEGE
HOMETOWN	INDEPENDENCE, MINNESOTA
JERSEY	N/A
POSITION	EVENT: 8K XC, STEEPLECHASE TRACK
FAVORITE ATHLETE	TEAMMATES AT WHEATON
FAVORITE MOVIE	THE MATRIX
FAVORITE ICE CREAM	HIS MOM'S HOMEMADE ICE CREAM
HOBBIES	TRYING NEW LANGUAGES, PARKOUR
RANDOM FACT	FAVORITE TV SHOW IS SPONGEBOB

WHY WORSHIP?

Even though I have graduated, I am still not sure why I started cross-country and track in college. I ran in high school, so I knew I could do it. But I asked myself why should I keep running for another step, another race, another year when it is so difficult. I believe our purpose on earth is to "fear God and keep His commandments" (Ecclesiastes 12:13). In the end, I found one true purpose to running and everything else: worship.

Freshman year, I was totally unprepared. I wanted to try one season just to make friends, but after finishing second to last on our team, I learned I would have to train harder than ever. Was it worth the pain? I was not sure. In my challenges, God encouraged me through amazing Christian teammates and coaches. They loved me for who I was, not how I ran. So I kept running.

During the next two years, I found value in running to encourage my teammates. Still, I pondered, "How does running matter in my relationship with God?" This question struck me almost every race.

I could keep pace with my teammates for two-thirds of the race, but when it got hard—lungs closing, muscles locking, vision fading—I found no real reason to keep going. I wondered if I could worship God through running. I knew to seek God above all else (Matthew 6:33), so I kept going.

I still remember the race. Senior year, we were running at St. James Farm, our home course. Same struggles. Same questions. But one difference: worship. Before every race, our coach would go over the race-day checklist with us: start time, competition, etc. But I never fully grasped the last thing he would always put on our checklist: worship.

The cross-country race at St. James changed that. It was not flashy, but God gave me the quiet realization that every step can be worship by offering thanks, acknowledging His reign, and giving Him all the glory. God made me joyful in worship even when I was unable to compete my last track season due to a broken foot. God set me free to "run in the path of His commands" in everything I do with Him (Psalm 119:32).

1. What is true worship? (See Micah 6:6-8, Psalm 51:17, 1 Corinthians 13)

"I have chosen the way of faithfulness; I have set my heart on your laws. I hold fast to your statutes, LORD; do not let me be put to shame. I run in the path of your commands, for you have broadened my understanding."

Psalm 119:30-32 (NIV)

79

KELSEY KRAMER

ROWING

UNIVERSITY  UNIVERSITY OF WISCONSIN MADISON

HOMETOWN KAUKAUNA, WISCONSIN

JERSEY N/A

POSITION N/A

FAVORITE ATHLETE AARON RODGERS AND RUSSELL WILSON

FAVORITE MOVIE REMEMBER THE TITANS

FAVORITE ICE CREAM  VANILLA

HOBBIES SAILING AND TRAVELING

RANDOM FACT HICCUPS AT LEAST ONCE A DAY

GOD'S PLAN > MY PLAN

When I was accepted to the University of Wisconsin–Madison, I knew I had big things in store for my future. My biggest mistake, however, was thinking I could handle the next four crucial years all on my own and make my own plans. I clearly needed a reality check.

With freshman year in full swing, I walked on to the rowing team and took a full course load. I felt like I was on top of the world and it could not get any better. I was constantly planning the next step and trying to meet the people who would help me get there. I tried to please coaches and meet professors.

Unfortunately, I strayed from my faith and did not consider God as someone who would help me succeed. By the end of freshman year, nothing was going according to my plan. I was not racing as much as I had hoped and my grades were less than ideal, which caused me to lose my academic scholarship.

The summer before sophomore year, I was angry. I made more plans to turn the next year around. In the fall, a teammate asked me to go to an organization with her called Athletes in Action. I figured, why not? I could meet people and put off doing homework, which were two of my favorite things. Little did I realize how much of a positive influence this group of people would have on me and my future.

I became aware of many athletes in situations similar to mine—life was not going according to plan. The answer they found was something I had put on the back burner for almost two years: God and faith. Since then, I have realized I cannot do anything on my own, no matter how hard I try. I must put my pride aside and admit that I need help. Life has not been perfect since I have come back to Christ and my faith, but things have been a lot simpler. My grades are up and competition has been easier, knowing I am competing for an audience of one. Becoming a Christian student athlete is one of the best changes I have made in my life.

1. Is your walk with God strong enough to allow the fulfillment of God's plan, even if it doesn't match your plan?

"Whatever you do, work at it with all your heart, as working for the Lord, not for human masters."

Colossians 3:23 (NIV)

80

MIKE CIMMARRUSTI

HOCKEY

UNIVERSITY	WHEATON COLLEGE
HOMETOWN	MICHIGAN
JERSEY	#16
POSITION	CENTER
FAVORITE ATHLETE	PAVEL DATSYUK
FAVORITE MOVIE	THE DARK KNIGHT
FAVORITE ICE CREAM	CHOCOLATE
HOBBIES	HOCKEY
RANDOM FACT	ONCE DID A BACKFLIP ON A DIRT BIKE

PLAYING FOR GOD

It was not until October of my freshman year that I realized what a blessing it was to go to Wheaton College. I had grown up going to public schools where Christianity was far from encouraged, if not frowned upon. Sports for me had always been set apart from my relationship with God, a separation of church and state, if you will. To be quite honest, my Christian walk had been less than significant for the majority of my high school career, so being engrossed in a Christian atmosphere was an adjustment.

Right before we hit the ice, our senior captain, Erik Russo, would remind us what we were playing for. It was not for ourselves and it was not for the team, it was for God. Two years earlier, those words would have had no meaning to me.

"Playing for God" was a phrase tossed around when I was a kid, but it never meant anything, at least not until God found me. At 17, I was running as far as I could from God, from Jesus, from everything. But a friend of mine Joe White laid the most convicting words on me I had ever heard.

"Michael, everything you do in this world is either taking people to the best place they could ever imagine or the WORST place they could imagine."

Wait a second. Joe was telling me that regardless of what I believed, everything I did affected others.

Those very words led to me abandon everything and run blissfully into the arms of my Creator. It was those words that made the phrase "playing for God" so important. It did not matter if I prayed with a guy after practice or shared the gospel over a cup of coffee or just played the game. Whatever I did was going to have an effect on someone, somewhere. So I resolved to mercilessly pursue a life that brings people to the greatest place they could ever picture. Will you do the same?

1. What is one way that you can change the way you play the game to influence others towards Christ?

"Live such good lives among the pagans that, though they accuse you of doing wrong, they may see your good deeds and glorify God on the day He visits us."

1 Peter 2:12 (NIV)

81

RON BROWN

UNIVERSITY	LIBERTY UNIVERSITY
HOMETOWN	NEW YORK, NEW YORK
JERSEY	N/A
POSITION	RECEIVERS COACH
FAVORITE ATHLETE	ERIC LIDDELL
FAVORITE MOVIE	CHARIOTS OF FIRE
FAVORITE ICE CREAM	GOLDEN VANILLA
HOBBIES	READING THE BIBLE
RANDOM FACT	GOD USED A COUPLE TO ADOPT HIM AND RESCUE HIM FROM A DIFFICULT LIFE.

ROOTED

The platform of influence that is granted to athletes and coaches in this great country can be a fruitful one. Every single day we have the opportunity to utilize our medium of athletics to impact lives and spread the Good News. This privilege is not without its trials, however.

John 15:20 tells us that if you are defending the faith, persecution is a virtual certainty. I cannot tell you how many times I have personally experienced this, but I can honestly sit here and tell you that it would be an honor to be fired for defending my faith. I would rather lose my job than denounce Jesus Christ.

Even if the world is not openly persecuting your faith, the culture here in America today has its own way of oppressing it. It has become the status quo to compartmentalize Christianity, relegating it to our churches on Sunday mornings and Wednesday nights. It is seen as abnormal and atypical to live out your faith every single day of the week, every single week of the year, every single year of your life. Sunday morning repentance for Saturday night transgressions has become far too common of a notion.

Like many folks in their youth, I started out this way as well. During my sophomore year of high school, I attended a local Bible study in my hometown and was encouraged to give my life to Jesus. But the desires and endeavors of this world got in the way and I went my own way for a while instead of God's, making academics and athletics my god instead.

I went on to play Ivy League football in college and as an undrafted free agent I had a cup of coffee with the Dallas Cowboys. But that fell apart. I vividly remember the day in 1979 that I started following Jesus. Since then, nothing has been the same. I'm using athletics to minister to those who were lost sheep just like me; I know that God has put me in this position to do that work. His work.

1. Would you consider it an honor to be fired for defending your faith?

"I will speak of your statutes before kings
and will not be put to shame."
Psalm 119:46 (NIV)

82

SAMANTHA MILLER

SOCCER

UNIVERSITY	MILLIKIN UNIVERSITY
HOMETOWN	WASHINGTON, ILLINOIS
JERSEY	#14, #27
POSITION	MIDFIELDER
FAVORITE ATHLETE	JULIE FOUDY AND YADIER MOLINA
FAVORITE MOVIE	SHES THE MAN AND LITTLE RASCALS
FAVORITE ICE CREAM	PEANUT BUTTER CUP
HOBBIES	HUNTING, FISHING, FOUR-WHEELING, BAKING
RANDOM FACT	HAS WHITE WATER RAFTED IN GRAND CANYON

PRESSING ON, THROUGH, AND INTO HIM

"You're going to have to take some time off."

My heart sunk to my toes.

I had been putting it off for months. I knew something was wrong with my foot, but it was a pain I could push through for the sake of playing the game I love. Finally the pain became constant. With every step I took, it seemed to get worse.

A few x–rays with the training staff and the doctor revealed that I had a stress fracture in a little bone in the ball of my foot. It was a tiny bone and a tiny stress fracture, but caused a ton of pain. It became clear that my protests were in vain; I'd have to hang it up for a while.

So began a long offseason of biking, swimming and daily bone growth treatment, and boot walking through snow. It was quite a trial. God was teaching me to rely on him in the midst of my frustration. People did not understand what was wrong. I had not had one of the "big" injuries, such as an ACL tear, a broken bone, or a severe ankle sprain. It was not visible, and people always gave me a hard time, even some of my teammates.

Then it got worse. While I was focusing so much attention on my left foot, I had acquired the same injury in my right foot in the process. I was beside myself. Luckily, I had some great influences on my life.

One of my assistant coaches met with me one day and I just broke down. He prayed for me and brought to me some verses regarding trials. From then on, I changed my perspective. I kept working to heal, knowing that God was using this experience to make me a stronger Christian and a better soccer player.

Trials are placed in our lives to test and strengthen us. I garnered a new appreciation for soccer because of it. Keep working through trials because you will come out with renewed resilience, and God will use it for HIS good, HIS purpose. Even when it does not make sense to you.

1. How can you praise God through the good and the bad?

"And we know that in all things God works together for the good of those who love him, who have been called according to his purpose."
Romans 8:28 (NIV)

83

MICHAEL AQUINO

BASEBALL

UNIVERSITY  RICE UNIVERSITY

HOMETOWN  THE WOODLANDS, TEXAS

JERSEY  #15

POSITION  DESIGNATED HITTER

FAVORITE ATHLETE  DEREK JETER AND ROBINSON CANO

FAVORITE MOVIE FOREST GUMP

FAVORITE ICE CREAM  CHOCOLATE AND VANILLA SWIRL

HOBBIES GUITAR AND DRUMS, WRITING SONGS

RANDOM FACT  NEVER SHOT A GUN BUT SITLL A TEXAN

JESUS, BASEBALL, AND THE LONG GRIND

Baseball, like many a sports, has the tendency to lift the spirits of a person to the highest point, then plunge them down quickly. Hours upon hours in hot pants are sacrificed daily in the blazing sun as you sweat through your batting gloves, trying with all of your might to master something you feel like you should know perfected already.

For me, that the blazing sun rises and falls in Houston, Texas, at Reckling Park, home of the Rice University baseball team. I felt like the whole world was handed to me when I was told that I had been accepted into Rice to be part of the baseball team. Doors were opened in many places, such as the opportunity to apply to medical school, thus following my father's path. I won a home run derby and a few championships along the way as well.

Everywhere I go, it seems, folks praise my play on the diamond. But they do not know that I struck out 56 times last season or how many times I let the game get in my head and set me up for failure.

Baseball is a game of failure and if you come to terms with that and push through, then you will be successful. It is so easy to get caught up with the praise, the success, and the failures of athletics, We often forget that our mission as athletes on and off the field should be one thing: not to gather up enough followers and fans for the sake of our own names, but rather to do so as to feed the bread of Jesus Christ. We all must realize from where your strength comes.

I have prayed before many at-bats for Jesus just to stand in the box with me and I ask of Him that if I do not get a hit this at-bat to at least protect me from harm. Just like baseball, life is a grind, but it's also a blessing. So grind it out letting everyone know, shout out everywhere you go, the power of Jesus' name.

1. How has Jesus been with you through your own "grind"?

"And hope does not put us to shame, because God's love has been poured out into our hearts through the Holy Spirit, who has been given to us."
Romans 5:5 (NIV)

84

NICHELLE GAEDDERT

BASKETBALL

UNIVERSITY	TRUMAN STATE UNIVERSITY
HOMETOWN	MCPHERSON, KANSAS
JERSEY	#24
POSITION	FORWARD
FAVORITE ATHLETE	STEPH CURRY
FAVORITE MOVIE	PITCH PERFECT
FAVORITE ICE CREAM	CHOCOLATE AND PEANUT BUTTER
HOBBIES	PLAYING PIANO AND READING
RANDOM FACT	USED TO BE INSECURE ABOUT BEING TALL BUT NOW SHE LOVES IT

UNEXPECTED PLANS

"All you can do now is take it one day at a time." These were the first words from my coach after the trainer told me I had torn my ACL. Needless to say, I was not prepared. I had worked all of preseason to come up short the practice before our first season game.

Life rarely turns out as we think it will and sports are no exception. Just when you think you know the best plan for your life, God comes in and works in unexpected ways. Sometimes, it seems His plan makes no sense at all.

Think about it: our Savior came as a child to a virgin, used five loaves of bread and two fish to feed five thousand people, raised the dead, rode a donkey and died alongside two criminals. Talk about unpredictable.

Even the Pharisees saw this man and did not believe because it was not "as planned." They missed out on the joy and wonder of God because it did not look the way they thought it should.

After a loss, an injury, or a bad practice it's easy for athletes to get so wrapped up in the pain and disappointment that we also miss out on our opportunity for something better.

God has a bigger plan for your life than you can ever imagine, and He states that in James 1:2. Do not miss out on the joy and the opportunities that come from your trials. Take it one day at a time and continue to see the good in everything.

1. How will you respond when God changes your plans?

"Then your light will break forth like the dawn, and your healing will quickly appear; then your righteousness will go before you, and the glory of the LORD will be your rear guard."
Isaiah 58:8 (NIV)

85

SETH CRUMPTON

FOOTBALL

UNIVERSITY 	MIDWESTERN STATE UNIVERSITY
HOMETOWN	HENRIETTA, TEXAS
JERSEY	#25
POSITION	SAFETY
FAVORITE ATHLETE	TIM TEBOW
FAVORITE MOVIE	THE AVENGERS AND WARRIOR
FAVORITE ICE CREAM 	COOKIES 'N CREAM
HOBBIES 	TOP GOLF AND FANTASY FOOTBALL
RANDOM FACT	FAVORITE SUPERHERO IS THE HULK

GET BACK UP

My high school senior season was something out of a storybook. Our team was undefeated and making history each week. As a quarterback, I received a ton of recognition for the success I had behind a solid line, backs and receivers. My dream of playing college football was becoming a reality. To someone on the outside, it seemed like I had everything. But the reality is that people couldn't see how lost I truly was. I literally watched every dream I had as a young athlete unfold right before my eyes, but I could not escape the feeling that something was missing.

There was a hole in my life, and no amount of success could make it disappear. I did not realize what the hole was until God brought a person into my life who was a light to me. After sharing Isaiah 40:31 with me when I needed it most, I could not help but think there was something truly special about this person.

Seeing more in me than just a football guy, this person invested in me and showed me what an example of Jesus Christ looked like. As a result, I embraced a walk with the Lord. The only problem was that I had not died to myself, so the old Seth was still there. Living a lie, I changed who I was depending on who I was around. When the truth came out, no one was more hurt than the person who had initially showed me the Lord.

For longer than I will admit, I hated myself for my actions. One night, in an act of desperation, I opened my Bible and buried myself in it. I found myself back in Isaiah 40:31 with two choices: give up or get back up. Finding strength in the verse, I began running to the cross and leaving the messy areas of my life behind. The harder I ran, the more the hole in my life faded. It became clear to me that this was what I had been missing. The realization helped me focus on the joy a relationship with Christ brings and I forgot about the emptiness I had felt.

Looking back, God blessed me with more than I deserved. He gave me a platform to show others my faith and I wasted it. Do not make the mistake I did. Games will comes and go, but nothing is more fulfilling than a relationship with Christ. What are you prepared to do with what Christ has given you?

1. What are you claiming in the game? Is it in route with the role you play on God's team?

"But those who hope in the LORD will renew their strength. They will soar on wings like eagles; they will run and not grow weary, they will walk and not be faint."

Isaiah 40:31 (NIV)

86

TINDALL SEWELL

VOLLEYBALL

UNIVERSITY	 	DAVIDSON COLLEGE
HOMETOWN		ATLANTA, GEORGIA
JERSEY		#13
POSITION		MIDDLE BLOCKER
FAVORITE ATHLETE		KERRI WALSH AND MISTY MAY
FAVORITE MOVIE		THE PROPOSAL
FAVORITE ICE CREAM		CHOCOLATE PEANUT BUTTER
HOBBIES		TRAVELING THE WORLD
RANDOM FACT		632 VOLLEYBALL CAREER KILLS

WHO'S IT ALL ABOUT?

Volleyball is the ultimate team sport. As a middle hitter, I hit the ball on third contact to finish the rally for a point. The crowd always cheers for a loud kill hit straight to the floor, but they often times forget to celebrate the incredible dig by a defensive specialist, or the setter's assist. Each position has a unique role and as teammates, we respect each other's talents. Personally, at 6'1" it's tough to get low for a pass. I am more adept at playing the net.

This embodies the body of Christ. As believers, He gives us different gifts to do certain things well, so that we all may come together and contribute to His glory.

We must identify our God-given gifts so that we can take ownership of our roles and put forth our best on a daily basis. Whether you are the quiet, hard worker on your team or the outgoing motivational speaker, every person is crucial. If everybody had the same gifts, the world would be a terribly boring and disproportional place. It does not matter if everyone is good at making a windshield if no one produces the car door.

I struggled with nagging injuries last season, something that I had to come to terms with. I lost my identity in playing time and the victory column, so I had to redefine myself in Christ alone.

My teammates often equate the concept of glorifying God to the phrase "Audience of One." Regardless if your teammates let you down or if your coach yells at you, God will never leave your side. If I am making proper use of the spiritual gifts that God gave me, then my actions throughout a match should reflect and glorify Jesus. We simply cannot fail because Christ has already declared victory for our lives through dying on the cross. He does not measure my life by statistics or the win column. Therefore, as believers we must freely accept our spiritual gifts from Christ, so that we may bring the best version of ourselves to the floor each day. Always giving your best effort. It's regret-proof, and you'll never be sorry.

1. What are your spiritual gifts and how can you identify them in others?

"For our light and momentary troubles are achieving for us an eternal glory that far outweighs them all."
2 Corinthians 4:17 (NIV)

87

MARY ARNOLD

TENNIS

UNIVERSITY  DEPAUW UNIVERSITY

HOMETOWN  EVANSVILLE, INDIANA

JERSEY N/A 

POSITION  DOUBLES AND SINGLES

FAVORITE ATHLETE MIA HAMM AND TIM TEBOW

FAVORITE MOVIE  MIRACLE

FAVORITE ICE CREAM PUMPKIN OR CHOCOLATE

HOBBIES  TRAVELING, READING THE BIBLE

RANDOM FACT  ONCE CONSIDERED BECOMING A NUN

EQUIPPED FOR HIS GLORY

I was not prepared. That is the best way to begin.

I played soccer my entire life, traveled on several select teams and loved my school teams. By my senior year of high school, college soccer was no longer a dream of mine. I was burned out. Where did my drive and love for soccer go? I was upset that my last season of soccer was not what I pictured. However, God had better plans for me than I did. Shortly after my soccer dreams disappeared, I was given a passion to play college tennis.

Since I did not play tennis as consistently as soccer, I knew it would take more than determination to play at the collegiate level. I needed strength and focus from the Lord.

As I entered my senior year of college, I knew that I was not equipped for tennis at an advanced level. However, my passion and new love for tennis drove me to practice, study the game, and prepare myself. I was not the best player and am still working up the ladder on our team; but my purpose is not to necessarily be the most successful on the court. It may sound unambitious, but my mission is to glorify God through my weaknesses and to share the love of Christ with my teammates and my competitors. What is not competitive about that, when we are facing a war with our soul?

The Lord equipped me to play college tennis because I am learning how to play in the biggest competition of my life—the spiritual war for people. God's purpose for me on the court might not be the most wins, but certainly it is to share His love with others and the victory already won by Him through His son, Jesus Christ. I was told God does not call the equipped, but He equips those called. I cling to that hope and trust that wherever God calls me, I will be prepared through His strength and not my own.

1. What weaknesses and strengths do you have that can be used to glorify the Lord?

"For we are God's handiwork, created in Christ Jesus to do good works, which God prepared in advance for us to do."
Ephesians 2:10 (NIV)

88

ERIC TERRAZAS

WRESTLING

UNIVERSITY — UNIVERSITY OF ILLINOIS

HOMETOWN — WHEATON, ILLINOIS

JERSEY — N/A

POSITION — WEIGHT CLASS: 149

FAVORITE ATHLETE — PETE SAMPRAS

FAVORITE MOVIE — REMEMBER THE TITANS

FAVORITE ICE CREAM — PEPPERMINT

HOBBIES — GOLF, BOWLING, GOING TO THE MOVIES

RANDOM FACT — WANTS TO COACH COLLEGE WRESTLING

NOAH: A MAN OF FAITH

Every week, in every church across America, we call our Lord and Savior many things. Forgiving. Compassionate. Righteous. While these terms certainly are on the right track, only one can adequately (and ironically) describe Him: Indescribable.

This being the case, it would make sense as well that faith in God would fit this mold. Hebrews 11:1, however, provides a few clues as to what characteristics of faith look like. It's important to note context when looking at this verse. In the first ten chapters of Hebrews, the author is explaining that the new covenant of grace (established by Christ's blood being shed on the cross) is superior to that of the old covenant. Faith is not a matter of works. Rather, it is a matter of grace.

The story of Noah perfectly exemplifies faith. God came to Noah and told him that it was going to rain. And not just rain any normal, fleeting shower; God said that this was going to be an ongoing affair. And to boot, up until this point, it had never rained; Noah didn't even have a clue what rain was. "How in the world was water going to fall from Heaven?", he probably thought. He must have pictured it a million times. But Noah trusted God, in spite of all of this, and God's promise to Noah came to fruition. It was one thing for Noah to dream what this would be like, but forming one's life around it is something else entirely. For the better part of 120 years, Noah built a boat in a desert! Building the ark didn't give Noah faith; rather, he built the ark because of his faith in God.

The kingdom of God shouldn't be any different in our lives. Because of the grace of God, we have been given the ability to believe and put our faith in Him. This faith is not just something that we are hoping is true; it is a reality in our lives, and contains substance. The Kingdom of God is real as well, and as such, we should give our lives up for it. He believed, he acted and he followed faithfully.

1. Every faithful person has their "Noah" story. What is yours?

"Now faith is confidence in what we hope for and assurance about what we do not see."
Hebrews 11:1 (NIV)

89

TIM DONDANVILLE

FOOTBALL

UNIVERSITY  PRINCETON UNIVERSITY

HOMETOWN  SPRINGFIELD, ILLINOIS

JERSEY  #5

POSITION 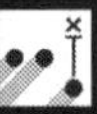 QUARTERBACK

FAVORITE ATHLETE  PEYTON MANNING AND DERRICK ROSE

FAVORITE MOVIE  SAVING PRIVATE RYAN

FAVORITE ICE CREAM  COOKIES 'N CREAM

HOBBIES  WATER SKIING, RUNNING, READING

RANDOM FACT  ONLY LEFT IN EXTENDED FAMILY OTHER THAN HIS AUNT

RESILIENT THROUGH HIM

Nobody likes change. Moving from Springfield, Illinois to Princeton, New Jersey was a very difficult change of scenery for me, both academically and athletically. In high school, I had little stress in regard to my classes and I was blessed to be part of three state championships under the tutelage of a well-established coaching staff. But during the week before Thanksgiving my freshman year at Princeton, I was in uncharted waters after failing a midterm and a 4-6 season that led to the sacking of my coaches.

When the new coaching staff arrived after Christmas break, they preached a tough-love philosophy that rubbed some of my teammates the wrong way. So much so, in fact, that over a third of my fellow freshmen quit the team. In addition, I was dealing with nagging hamstring issues and continued academic struggles. By the end of my sophomore season and a dismal 1-9 campaign, I was having serious doubts about whether I could cut it as a Princeton Tiger. I had never experienced adversity like this before (I had not ever lost nine football games in my whole life), and I contemplated quitting the team.

Just when I was going to prematurely end my career, my beloved uncle passed away after a long battle with cancer. At that point, football was the last thing on my mind; comforting my family became priority number one. The challenges at school seemed so small in perspective. My uncle was a caring husband, dedicated father, esteemed attorney, and an avid outdoorsman. He told me to laugh everything off and remember that I played because of my love for the game.

When I returned to school, I focused on my uncle's advice. Being a college student-athlete is difficult in general, but when you dedicate your life to God and the family that He has provided, your various trials will give way to a steadfast spirit.

1. Which people in your life can you serve as a role model?

"Consider it pure joy, my brothers and sisters, whenever you face trials of many kinds, because you know that the testing of your faith produces perseverance."
James 1:2-3 (NIV)

91

WES CUMMINS

SOCCER

UNIVERSITY  QUACHITA BAPTIST UNIVERSITY

HOMETOWN  CONWAY, ARKANSAS

JERSEY #16

POSITION CENTER-BACK

FAVORITE ATHLETE CLINT DEMPSEY AND LANDON DONOVAN

FAVORITE MOVIE STAR WARS

FAVORITE ICE CREAM COOKIES 'N CREAM

HOBBIES  COUNTRY FESTIVALS AND CONCERTS

RANDOM FACT MARRIED TO THE WOMAN OF HIS DREAMS

GOING IN GODS DIRECTION

Soccer, the world's favorite sport, (well, maybe not here in America) was my passion. It can be the most exciting game to watch, but also the most boring. Soccer is also one of the most physically demanding sports. The only protection for your body is shin guards and the game requires playing in many weather conditions: one–hundred–degree heat to freezing cold. Soccer has the ability to wear your body down to the point of no longer being able to play. That is what happened to me.

It started my senior year of high school, which was filled with many hardships. During preseason, I fractured my foot and tore my hamstring, both on the same leg. But that did not stop me from playing the sport that I love. I kind of lost my faith that year and was starting to ask God the question that everybody seems to ask: "Why is this happening to me?"

Before the injuries, everything was going great in my life, or so I thought. I was getting noticed by some great Division I schools to play center–back on the soccer team. But those opportunities all seemed to fade away into the background.

Not really knowing what to do, I turned to one of my mentors, Cory. After prayer and talking with Cory, I finally realized that God was telling me that I was going in the opposite direction of what He desired for me. I sat down and listened to Him, and ended up where He had wanted me to be the whole time. Unfortunately, my soccer career never made it past freshman year of college, but I do feel like God has placed me at the university I am at for a reason: to share His word and expand His Kingdom.

1. How can you use your misfortunes to further God's kingdom?

"Trust in the LORD with all your heart and lean not on your own understanding; in all your ways submit to him, and he will make your paths straight."
Proverbs 3:5-6 (NIV)

92

RYAN TALLEY

BASEBALL

UNIVERSITY	UNIVERSITY OF TEXAS AT SAN ANTONIO
HOMETOWN	ALEDO, TEXAS
JERSEY	#14
POSITION	PITCHER
FAVORITE ATHLETE	NOLAN RYAN
FAVORITE MOVIE	GLADIATOR
 FAVORITE ICE CREAM	PEANUT BUTTER GELATO
HOBBIES	CROSSFIT
RANDOM FACT 	LOVES ALMOND BUTTER

IF IT WAS EASY, EVERYONE WOULD DO IT

Imagine a school of fish in the ocean. They were all swimming in the same direction, just going with the current. But one fish decided he wanted to go the other direction. He knew that the school was headed straight into the direction of a great white shark.

Although a cheesy scenario, this is the exact situation that many of us find ourselves in daily. The question is, do you want to turn your life/career in the right direction, are you going to take action, be bold, and not let others push you in other directions? The fact of the matter is, when it comes to sports, faith, or anything else, the non-committed, mediocre, short-cutters in life will always try to drag you down to their level, so that they can justify their subpar actions.

Therefore I urge you, do not live your life aiming to please others, because man will never be pleased. No matter how good you are, they will always want more. Rather, take joy in understanding Matthew 5:10; fully expecting and accepting the mockery and ridicule that you will receive, if the less traveled road is the one chosen.

I can testify that in my own life it was not until I embraced being different (1 Peter 2:11) that I began to feel more confident and experienced more success both on the field and in my walk with God. I was no longer seeking man's approval, but God's. The beauty of it all is this: when you come to bumps in the road, which come to everyone at one time or another (bad games, bad coaches, not enough playing time, end of career), we now have confidence and maturity to thank God, learn from it and move on. That is one of the hardest things to do. I know, because when things did not go my way, I got angry, which lead to nothing of value.

The next time you find yourself in a situation where everyone is telling you how you should act and feel, but you know better, consider Matthew 5:10, and remember, "If it was easy, everyone would do it."

1. Do you want to store up for yourself treasures on earth, or in heaven?

"Blessed are those who have been persecuted for the sake of righteousness, for theirs is the kingdom of heaven."

Mathew 5:10 (NIV)

93

TREVOR CONNER

FOOTBALL

UNIVERSITY SOUTHWEST BAPTIST UNIVERSITY

HOMETOWN OWASSO, OKLAHOMA

JERSEY #34

POSITION SAFETY

FAVORITE ATHLETE MARCUS MARIOTA

FAVORITE MOVIE RUDY

FAVORITE ICE CREAM ANDY'S BANANA

HOBBIES HANGING WITH FRIENDS, FAMILY, AND WIFE

RANDOM FACT CONSTANTLY SINGS WHEN NO ONE IS AROUND

CONTENTMENT: GOD'S STAKE IN YOUR LIFE

Sometimes we look at our lives and say "I wish..." or "If only...". Sometimes we find ourselves struggling with doubt and uncertainty, looking everywhere for truth when it seems to be so very absent. Sometimes we struggle and that is just the truth of it all. Then there are times that everything seems to be going well and you are just breezing along to success. Whatever may apply to you at the moment, it is certain that something you have yet to encounter will change it all. Your disposition as to how you view reality will be decided in large part by your experiences.

So how does anyone find contentment in the midst of a life that guarantees only change and worldly disappointment? When I was a senior at SBU, I struggled to find playing time in the midst of what appeared to be a hypocritical coaching staff. I was also struggling with doubt in my personal relationships that were very dear to my heart. All of this being said, it was very difficult to be content, for I was being torn in every which direction but the truth. It was as if all I knew in my life to be true, good, and built upon love was being challenged at its very core. In my quest for answers I ran across this quote: "Remember this, had any other condition been better for you than the one in which you are, divine love would have put you there." – C.H. Spurgeon

This is not an easy concept to grasp for the minds of many a man. Naturally, our sinful nature is opposed to such an idea. Therefore, it will take time for you to fully understand this, that contentment is a choice and it must be learned, It must be embraced by each one of us. Make no mistake, everything in our lives happens for a reason and that reason is ultimately good in our Father who has willed it. Disregard the lies of the enemy and of your flesh and truly be satisfied with the good lot the Father has bestowed upon you!

1. In what ways can you alter your mindset to embrace the integrity and righteousness of God in your life in order that you may know that everything, every situation, every person, every relationship, every disaster, every moment, is orchestrated by our Father to be the utmost good of our souls?

"I am not saying this because I am in need, for I have learned to be content whatever the circumstances."
Philippians 4:11 (NIV)

94

WALKER TUTEN

BASKETBALL

UNIVERSITY	BERRY COLLEGE
HOMETOWN	ROSWELL, GEORGIA
JERSEY	#14
POSITION	SHOOTING GUARD
FAVORITE ATHLETE	HERSCHEL WALKER
FAVORITE MOVIE	THE BOURNE IDENTITY
FAVORITE ICE CREAM	MILK AND COOKIES
HOBBIES	BASKETBALL
RANDOM FACT	WAS ON SPORTSCENTER

HOW MANY MORE FLAGS DO YOU GOT?

Anger is deeply intertwined into modern day athletics. It is common to see a big leaguer get ejected after arguing a call. Technical fouls are a regular occurrence for many NBA players and NFL players talking trash after just about every play, it seems. Yet, all through The Good Book, God calls us to be slow to anger:

1. We should do so because it is Christ–like; God himself is slow to anger. (Ephesians 5:1). Therefore, if God is slow to anger, we should be too. Key verses: Psalm 86:15, Psalm 145:8.
2. Being slow to anger resolves conflict. Responding to adversity in a calm manner is always more effective. Despite the fact that this is an accepted societal phenomenon, the practice of which remains ever uncommon. Key verse: Proverbs 15:18.
3. Anger accomplishes nothing. It tears apart rapport and relationships, and we usually justify it as "righteous anger" when we feel that we've been wronged. Key verse: James 1:19-20.

For years, losing composure on the basketball court was a major issue for me. Searching for an entity to blame, the most convenient of which was the referees. I would not have to change in the locker room with them or sit next to them on the bus if I abused them. This resulted in the occasional technical foul and a negative example for Christ as well. Although I realized that getting angry served no purpose and that I was not bringing God glory by doing so, this did not change my demeanor. I masked the issue under the "I'm just really competitive" mantra.

The root of it all was that I cared more about on–court success than witnessing for Christ. From that point on, I constantly prayed that God would give me the strength to glorify Him through my play, and that I would put Him first, always.

1. Instead of becoming angry, what are some more fruitful things that you can do when you feel like you have been wronged?

"Whoever is patient has great understanding, but one who is quick–tempered displays folly."

Proverbs 14:29 (NIV)

95

MIKE MONAGHAN

LACROSSE

UNIVERSITY — UNIVERSITY OF MISSOURI

HOMETOWN  — DARIEN, ILLINOIS

JERSEY  — #19

POSITION  — DEFENSIVE MIDFEILD, FACE OFF SPECIALIST

FAVORITE ATHLETE  — JONATHAN TOEWS AND JAKE HERBERT

FAVORITE MOVIE  — ANCHORMAN

FAVORITE ICE CREAM  — BLUE MOON

HOBBIES  — FISHING, WORKING THE FARM, RUNNING

RANDOM FACT  — LOVES COOKING FOR PEOPLE

PLAY FOR HIM

My freshman year was a colossal on–field success. We were first in our conference and we won almost every game. But the same could hardly be said for my sophomore campaign. Thus far, I had been playing for myself and putting lacrosse in front of everything, even God. But getting involved with Fellowship of Christian Athletes taught me a multitude of things, namely that God's greatness cannot be measured, as are the good things that He provides. I started looking at Jeremiah 32:26-27 and thinking, "It's amazing how He is in control at all times, therefore we can accomplish all. He is my Lord and Savior, and I need Him. I need His presence."

I did my best to change the team's culture by myself, lacking faith in God all the while. After I changed my approach, however, slowly the team began to change, and we made the playoffs to boot. I wholeheartedly believe that leading through adversity and the constant faithful prayer put forth contributed to these triumphs in a huge way.

No matter what you are up against, be it something small like the motivation to study for a test, or something monumental such as curing a family member of cancer, nothing is too big when God is in the picture (which is all the time, as He is eternally all–knowing). Take the time to speak to God. He never stops listening.

1. Is God your top priority or have you placed your faith in worldy desires?

"Then the LORD came to Jeremiah: 'I am the LORD, the God of all mankind. Is anything too hard for me?'"
Jeremiah 32:26-27 (NIV)

96-97

TANNER-TYLER SIMON

GOLF

UNIVERSITY	OUACHITA BAPTIST UNIVERSITY
HOMETOWN	DENTON, TEXAS
JERSEY	N/A
POSITION	N/A
FAVORITE ATHLETE	ALL TEXAS RANGERS; TIM TEBOW
FAVORITE MOVIE	HARRY POTTER, THE DARK KNIGHT
FAVORITE ICE CREAM	CHOCOLATE CHIP
HOBBIES	BASEBALL; ANYTHING OUTDOORS
RANDOM FACT	WATCHES EVERY RANGERS GAME; THEY HAVE OFTEN BEEN MISTAKEN FOR TRIPLETS

WHEN LIFE GIVES YOU BOGIES

Flashing back to when my brother and I were 10—we were at a sleepover and had come home the next day to find out our father, always a picture of health, had been hospitalized and was on his deathbed due to drastically low blood pressure.

During that time, my brother and I were forced to grow up way too fast. We practically lived in the hospital, but in time we began to look "through his eyes," into his perspective. In the five years that followed, my father was pronounced dead twice, but twice he was brought back to life by the grace of God. This was not without consequences, however. He was diagnosed with Alzheimer's disease at the age of 40 and placed on disability. Growing up and seeing a loved one go through all of this misery, not knowing if you will be remembered the next morning is a tough. At first we thought "Why? Why us?" Which soon then turned into "Why is God putting us through this?" Put simply, we questioned our faith. Nevertheless, we passed through these trials and tribulations, gaining a better appreciation for God's plans all the while.

Now my father is on a strict medical regimen, taking a handful of pills every morning and every night. The disease is debilitating, slowly preventing his brain from forming new memories and retrieving old ones; but this does not stop my dad from living. We will always look up to our parents for the courage and perseverance they have displayed.

Romans 14:8 means so much to me because I know that God has a plan, even if it remains unknown to us. It is very clear in the mind of the Lord, however; what other joy do we need?

1. What is your plan? Is it a selfish one? Look through His eyes to find out.

"For if we live, we live for the Lord; and if we die, we die for the Lord. So, whether we live or die, we belong to the Lord."
Romans 14:8 (NIV)

98

WADE PELC

FOOTBALL

UNIVERSITY	TRUMAN STATE UNIVERSITY
HOMETOWN	STROMSBURG, NEW ENGLAND
JERSEY	#45
POSITION	LINEBACKER
FAVORITE ATHLETE	RAY LEWIS AND REX BURKHEAD
FAVORITE MOVIE	INCEPTION
FAVORITE ICE CREAM	EGG NOG
HOBBIES	GUITAR, VIDEO GAMES, CHASING HIS DOG
RANDOM FACT	NEVER SKIPS LEG DAY

NEVER BRING A SWORD TO A PEBBLE FIGHT

As a football player and Christian, there is a constant struggle between the masculinity that is a required in football and the gentleness we are accustomed to believing is associated with being a Christian. We are told to be loving, kind-hearted, and never maim someone's character. Many times we pass up opportunities to witness because we do not want to offend anyone.

As I entered college, I acted as if football and my faith were separate, each to be done in their own time. As I grew closer to the Lord, however, I felt conflicted as to how to challenge my fellow man in a way that displayed my faith. How assertive should I be? Will I lose credibility if I confront their lifestyle? What if I slip up and I'm labeled a faker? There were also moments where I justified not giving my best to Christ.

The world is spinning its own story and creating its own rules. Men and women start to create their own perceptions of the world when they get into college and there is no room for being soft. We are called to be sanctified and set apart from the world in order to do His will, something that no person could do without God's help.

One way to examine the true heart of God is exploring who He uses to accomplish His goals and show His power. The greatest and most well-known example of this is in the story of David and Goliath. David confronted Goliath with nothing but a slingshot and a few pebbles. He bore no armor. He carried no sword. He sported no shield. But he had God on his side and that is why the smallest and the youngest of Goliath's forty six challengers was also the one to vanquish him.

God uses people who are ready to attack His work, whether it is against Goliath, sin, or the hearts of those to whom you can minister. We must be prepared to attack relentlessly. We must all be the modern-day David and fight back against Satan for the glory of Him.

1. How can you best stick up for God and fight for His honor?

"David said to the Philistine, 'You come against me with sword and spear and javelin, but I come against you in the name of the LORD Almighty, the God of the armies of Israel, whom you have defied.'"
1 Samuel 17:45 (NIV)

99

MEGAN WITASZAK

CHEER

UNIVERSITY	BAYLOR UNIVERSITY
HOMETOWN	OVERLAND PARK, KANSAS
JERSEY	N/A
POSITION	N/A
FAVORITE ATHLETE	PEYTON MANNING AND DERRICK ROSE
FAVORITE MOVIE	SWEET HOME ALABAMA
FAVORITE ICE CREAM	CHOCOLATE CHIP COOKIE DOUGH
HOBBIES	RUNNING, TRAVELING, EVENT PLANNING
RANDOM FACT	CAN RECITE THE ALPHABET BACKWARDS

SUPPORT BEHIND THE SPORT

When I look back on the last few years, I am unable to fully grasp the opportunities that God has laid before me: Robert Griffin III torching opponents during his Heisman trophy run; Brittney Griner crushing NCAA records; Brady Heslip burying nine 3-pointers in a game. I have been blessed to cheer them all.

In high school, I never thought I would be cheerleading for a Division I school in the Big 12 or being afforded the opportunity to travel the country for March Madness and meet the likes of Trace Adkins and George Bush.

Time and time again, cheerleaders are told that what they are doing is not a sport. And the crazy thing is, I have to agree. It is so much more. Cheerleading is not a sport. It's support. This play on words has given me a greater perspective regarding the purpose of what I do. We are to encourage and urge players to do their best. And we, as Christians, are called to do this very same thing.

We are all in this same game of life, playing for the same team, headed in the same direction. Just as in any athletic contest, there are always going to be unfair calls and tough setbacks. It is important to remember that life as a Christian is not guaranteed to be easy and fair. It is only promised to be worth it. A team is only as strong as the bonds within it. Encouragement is huge when building those bonds.

As Christians, we need to be the ones lifting each other up. It's not just the duty of a select few; it is asked of all of us, every day.

1. What are you doing to spur others on in their walks with the Lord?

"And let us consider how we may spur one another on toward love and good deeds, not giving up meeting together, as some are in the habit of doing, but encouraging one another—and all the more as you see the Day approaching."

Hebrews 10:25 (NIV)

100

SAMMY LUTZ

GYMNASTICS

UNIVERSITY	TOWSON UNIVERSITY
HOMETOWN	MURFREESBORO, TENNESSEE
JERSEY	N/A
POSITION	FAV EVENT: UNEVEN BARS
FAVORITE ATHLETE	STEPH CURRY
FAVORITE MOVIE	MR. MAGORIUM'S WONDER EMPORIUM
FAVORITE ICE CREAM	PISTACHIO
HOBBIES	HIKING AND TRAVELING
RANDOM FACT	LIVED IN THE SAME HOUSE HER ENTIRE LIFE PRIOR TO COMING TO COLLEGE

IN MY WEAKNESS I HAVE STRENGTH

The verses below make me think of going through hard workouts during preseason. Imagine your own preseason workouts. You push yourself to exhaustion and give everything you have got, to be able to finish stronger than you began. Think of a time during those workouts when you felt weak, like you could not give any more, you could not push any longer. Where did your mind go at that moment? Did you remember your purpose? Did you think about the fact that in your weaknesses, God is your strength? Or did you, like many others, including myself, think you could not go on and start to pity yourself by saying you could not do it?

When I read this verse, one particular experience comes to mind. We were out on the football field doing our usual Sunday circuit. It was toward the end of the workout, the last exercise before being done for the day. The task at hand was to carry a teammate on my back for the perimeter of the field twice. So, my teammate jumped on my back and I started to walk. I hit my point of exhaustion about halfway around the field the first time. All I could think about was wanting to stop. Then, a phrase popped into my mind: "In my weakness you are my strength." This changed my focus from wanting to stop to wanting to keep going. I continued saying that for the rest of that lap and all through the second lap around the field. It is truly amazing what strength God gives us if we choose to focus on Him and place our hope in Him rather than other distractions in our lives.

Putting our hope in the Lord opens up so many opportunities we never would have seen before. Who does not want to "soar on wings like eagles…run and not grow weary… walk and not be faint"? The Lord will show us how to put our hope in Him for every aspect of life, if we ask Him.

1. How can I remind myself to place my hope in the Lord during struggles?

"He gives strength to the weary and increases the power of the weak. Even youths grow tired and weary, and young men stumble and fall; but those who hope in the LORD will renew their strength. They will soar on wings like eagles; they will run and not grow weary, they will walk and not be faint."

Isaiah 40:29-31 (NIV)

101

ZETH BARRON

FOOTBALL

UNIVERSITY: HARDIN-SIMMONS UNIVERSITY

HOMETOWN: EASTLAND, TEXAS

JERSEY: #41 STRONG SAFETY

POSITION: POLE VAULT, JAVELIN, 100M, 200M

FAVORITE ATHLETE: EMMITT SMITH AND ADRIAN PETERSON

FAVORITE MOVIE: THE DARK KNIGHT

FAVORITE ICE CREAM: VANILLA

HOBBIES: GUITAR, DRUMS, SINGING, HUNTING

RANDOM FACT: TAUGHT HIMSELF GUITAR IN 7TH GRADE

FISH FOR HIM

Being a college athlete, it is no secret that I really enjoy sports and competition. I have always liked football and pole-vaulting the most. I have spent countless hours practicing and competing at these sports. What I have noticed being an athlete is that you can always tell who truly is passionate about what they do by how much time and effort they put into to it. Matthew 6:21 says, "For where your treasure is, there your heart will be also."

Before Simon Peter was a disciple of Jesus Christ, he was merely a fisherman. He probably enjoyed fishing as much as I enjoy football. After Jesus had died and had risen, Simon Peter and the other disciples did not know what else to do besides returning to what they had done before; so Simon Peter and a couple other disciples went out fishing. Jesus then appeared to them and invited them to share breakfast.

Upon eating, Jesus asked Peter an important question, "Do you love Me more than these?" Jesus was asking Simon Peter if he loved Him more than the fish they were eating. I too constantly have to pose this question to myself. Do I truly love Jesus more than the sports that I am passionate about, or is this meaningless dialogue instead?

In John 21:15 Jesus lays out a clear direction for how we should conduct our lives. He commands us to feed His lambs, meaning we are to use our passions and talents for Him, and Him only. Jesus is calling us to demonstrate our love for Him. It is a call to action, not a call to speak.

1. What are you truly most passionate about?

"When they had finished eating, Jesus said to Simon Peter, "Simon son of John, do you love me more than these?..."
John 21:15 (NIV)

102

EMILY MITAL

BASKETBALL

UNIVERSITY — UNIVERSITY OF MASSACHUSETTS AMHERST

HOMETOWN  — FRISCO, TEXAS

JERSEY — #24

POSITION — SHOOTING GUARD

FAVORITE ATHLETE — RICH FRONING

FAVORITE MOVIE — ELF

FAVORITE ICE CREAM — CHOCOLATE PEANUT BUTTER

HOBBIES — COACHING

RANDOM FACT — HAS A HEART SHAPED BIRTH MARK

SHOOTING FOR PERFECTION

As long as I can remember, I have been a perfectionist. Everything I did, it had to be flawless. When I picked up a basketball, I carried this attitude over to the court. I wanted to play a perfect game, shoot a high percentage, and never turn the ball over. In college, I struggled with disappointment from never meeting my expectations and I feared failing. This hindered my performance on the court. I experienced a 6-week shooting slump in the middle of season. For those of you who do not know basketball terms, I could not make an outside jumpshot to save my life! My mental attitude toward the game slowly got worse and worse.

Making outside shots was one of my only roles as a teammate and I was failing miserably. I tried to fix my shot by making more baskets daily. I shot for hours on end, day after day after day. I laid in bed at night envisioning myself making 3 point baskets. I played shooting games with our managers to try to make basketball fun again. It seemed like the more I tried to succeed, the more I failed. What I did not realize was that the perfection I was aiming for was the human standard. I did not comprehend that I was made perfect in Christ. The perfectionists in the Bible were the Pharisees, who were viewed as prideful, judgmental, and hypocritical. Perfectionism stems from personal pride, and God calls us to be humble in His name, not prideful of the human flesh. In fact, perfection on earth is a myth. It cannot be achieved or sustained unless, of course, your name is Jesus Christ. 2 Corinthians 12:9 states that God's grace is enough to make me perfect in His eyes. If we hand our weaknesses over to Christ and surrender our aim to live up to human standards, we can fully experience His power.

Through this verse, I realized that in wanting to have a perfect shooting performance, I was trying to please man, rather than playing to honor God alone. God does not care whether we score 30 points or not, in fact, nothing about our statistics is relevant to God. We should only care about honoring Him through our play, and surrendering ourselves to His power and grace. This truly freed me on the court. I slowly learned to put away my performance-driven attitude and dwell on my image in Christ, rather than my image as a basketball player. As athletes, we can all learn to give our weaknesses to God and live in His grace. Instead of attempting to live up to human standards and failing again and again, let's strive to free ourselves of the bondage of perfection and remember that only God's opinion of us matters.

1. Are you finding yourself performance driven lately or Christ-driven?

"But he said to me, "My grace is sufficient for you, for my power is made perfect in weakness. Therefore, I will boast all the more gladly about my weaknesses, so that Christ's power may rest on me."

2 Corinthians 12:9 (NIV)

103

SALLY HIGGINS

BASKETBALL

UNIVERSITY — WEST TEXAS A&M UNIVERSITY

HOMETOWN — ST. ANGELO, TEXAS

JERSEY — #12

POSITION — SHOOTING GUARD

FAVORITE ATHLETE — MAYA MOORE

FAVORITE MOVIE — REMEMBER THE TITANS

FAVORITE ICE CREAM — BLUE BELL COOKIES 'N CREAM

HOBBIES — READING AND HANGING OUT WITH FRIENDS

RANDOM FACT — DOESN'T LIKE TAKING NAPS

DISCIPLINE

I was a hooper from a very young age. Basketball has been a game I've adored my whole life. When I was young, my dad and brother would always tell me, "If you work hard you could play on varsity as a freshman." As I grew older it became, "You could win a state championship," then "You could get a scholarship to play college ball." A good work ethic was instilled in me at a very young age, and has become a very important attribute to me. It's something that I believe is of enormous significance, not just in athletics but in all of life. Therefore, I have noticed that my discipline has been something that people have begun to identify me by. While my sinful pride is tempted to puff up at such an attribution, the Lord has gracefully convicted my heart and opened my eyes to greater truth.

God then began to open my eyes to how passionate He is about His people living lives that are pleasing to Him. Ephesians tells us that "He chose us in Him before the foundation of the world that we should be holy and blameless before Him" (Ephesians 1:4). In the midst of a culture that tells us how we should act, what's an acceptable and normal way to behave, the Lord calls us to a higher standard for the sake of His great purpose. It was the same when Paul was writing a letter to the Phililppians. He tells them that God is at work in them for His good pleasure so "that you may prove yourselves to be blameless and innocent children of God, above reproach in the midst of a crooked and perverse generation, among whom you appear as lights in the world" (Philippians 2:13, 15).

Now please don't make the mistake in thinking I'm saying you should follow a list of rules on how to live your life. On the contrary, we were created as a people for His possession; zealous for good deeds (Titus 2:14) so that the world would see the great hope we have in a gracious and redeeming God. We are most satisfied in Him when He is most glorified in us. That's what Jesus meant when He said He came that we might have abundant life (John 10:10), because that abundant life is found in Him and not in anything of this world. If you continue reading on in our passage in 1 Timothy, verse 10 tells us the reason for being disciplined in our striving, "because we have fixed our hope on the living God, who is the Savior of all men, especially of believers." He offers a narrow path that leads to greater joy. So I encourage you, by the grace of God our King to take the narrow path and be diligent in seeking Him above all things.

1. What does it mean to be disciplined for the purpose of godliness?

"For physical training is of some value, but godliness has value for all things, holding promise for both the present life and the life to come."
1 Timothy 4:8 (NIV)

THRIVE U

ALEX DEMCZAK

A former quarterback for the Missouri Tigers from 2011-2015. Alex graduated with a degree in Communication and a minor in Business. He has a knack for starting new things such as Thrive U, Coach's Corner, MU Courtesy Carts, and Ignite small group at Mizzou. Alex plans on coaching college football and hopes to produce more books in the near future!

"Thrive U is a great resource for any athlete looking to grow in their faith. I highly recommend it!"

-JORDAN NORWOOD, NFL RECEIVER: DENVER BRONCOS

"In today's society so many athletes go through the motions. If you are someone who wants to Thrive, you need to read this book!"

-KYLE MCCLELLAN, MLB PITCHER

CONNECT WITH THRIVE U

WWW.THRIVEUATHLETES.COM

INSTAGRAM: @THRIVEU

TWITTER: @THRIVEUATHLETES

FACEBOOK: THRIVE U

Made in the USA
Lexington, KY
07 July 2016